IMAGES
of America

TACOMA'S
WATERFRONT

STEAMER "TACOMA."
FAST PASSENGER BOAT ON
TACOMA-SEATTLE RUN

Two early ships were christened with the name Tacoma. One, the USS *Tacoma*, was part of the navy's Great White Fleet. The passenger ferry *Tacoma* was launched on May 13, 1913, and remained in service until 1938, running up to 1,000 individuals a trip from the Tacoma Municipal Dock to Seattle. After 1928, when the Tacoma-to-Seattle highway opened, the steamer lost its popularity to the automobile.

ON THE COVER: Even though Tacoma was a product of the Northern Pacific Railroad, more than any other reality, lumber mills, ships, and Commencement Bay made the City of Destiny what it is today. The three elements are combined on the dock of the St. Paul and Tacoma Lumber Company where its crane loads finished timber onto the freighter *Tillamook*.

IMAGES
of America

TACOMA'S
WATERFRONT

Caroline Gallacci and Ron Karabaich

ARCADIA
PUBLISHING

Published by Arcadia Publishing
Charleston, South Carolina

Library of Congress Catalog Card Number: 2006930226

For all general information contact Arcadia Publishing at:
Telephone 843-853-2070
Fax 843-853-0044
E-mail sales@arcadiapublishing.com
For customer service and orders:
Toll-Free 1-888-313-2665

Visit us on the Internet at www.arcadiapublishing.com

To Ron Magden, our historian knight in shining armor.

CONTENTS

ACKNOWLEDGMENTS

Without the Tacoma Public Library Northwest Room's photograph collections, this history would not have been written. Through the glories of its Web site, it is possible to roam through thousands of images, complete with the historical background needed to detail the rather complex history of the Port of Tacoma. Space requirements for this history do now allow a complete numerical reference for the photographs provided by the library. These are in both the author's and the Tacoma Public Library files. In addition to the library's resources, the collections of coauthor Ron Karabaich, Thomas R. Stenger, and Jim Frederickson were equally valuable. Ron's photographs and Tom's extensive collection of Thomas H. Rutter images form a second major part of this waterfront history. Jim has spent all of his long life photographing and writing the history of local railroads.

As a historian who can never remember dates, Caroline Gallacci found her chronology in *The City of Destiny and the South Sound* (2001) useful in capturing those pesky numbers. *To Live in Dignity: Pierce County Labor, 1883–1989*, compiled by the Pierce County Labor Centennial Committee in 1989, is a valuable resource on the maritime and industrial unions. Murray Morgan's *Puget's Sound: A Narrative History of Early Tacoma and the Southern Sound* (1979) and Thomas Emerson Riply's *Green Timber* (1968) are both useful guides to Tacoma's past.

Ronald Magden and A. D. Martinson in *The Working Waterfront: The Story of Tacoma's Ships and Men* (1982) provide the best—and only—history of Tacoma's industrial port. As the historian's historian, Dr. Magden will always be our inspiration, and for that reason we dedicate this book to him.

INTRODUCTION

When, in the early years of the 1870s, banker Jay Cooke was pondering whether or not to finance the construction of the Northern Pacific Railroad line from Lake Superior to Puget Sound, he sent his trusted advisor Sam Wilkeson to survey the economic potential of the landscape. Wilkeson raved about the wonders he saw. Commencement Bay was "the Mediterranean of the Pacific Northwest," suggesting that he was here on a warm, sunny day. Wilkeson noted the deep water and reported it ideal for commerce. He witnessed the operations of the lumber mills scattered throughout Puget Sound, including the new Hanson, Ackerson Mill near a settlement called Tacoma City. And he surveyed the south shore of Commencement Bay along with the tidelands then owned only by the United States. Wilkeson reported back to Jay Cooke that financing a transcontinental railroad line would be a great investment, and in July 1873, the Northern Pacific board of directors selected a two-mile stretch of bay south of Tacoma City as its Puget Sound terminus.

The railroad company's intent was not to create a city, although one would be necessary. That task was left to the Tacoma Land Company along with a wide array of individual land speculators, businessmen and women large and small, investors, politicians, and their families. The relationship between the first Tacomans and the Northern Pacific was not always an amicable one, especially when it came to development along the shoreline. While the earliest city fathers and mothers assumed that when the railroad came the company would economically help the infant city along, the Northern Pacific was not the least bit interested. It viewed its task within its own economic context of transport and commerce. Produce and people were to be transferred from its trains to the ships that tied up to its wharves on Commencement Bay. In the beginning, Tacoma did not have a passenger depot downtown, Tacoma's waterfront was not Tacoma's, and the City Waterway was not the city's in spite of its name.

The importance of developing the Commencement Bay shoreline was never in doubt, however, and the purpose of this history is to provide a brief sketch as to how it all came about. The story told here is a complex and complicated one that starts with the Northern Pacific's terminal wharf constructed in 1873 and ends a century later, just before the Port of Tacoma began to reshape its facilities to accommodate container cargoes.

By the time the railroad arrived, Point Defiance had been set aside for the military, and Browns Point was a part of the Puyallup Indian Reservation. In turn, the entire reservation, which extended along the north shore of Commencement Bay across the delta to the Puyallup River, was technically within the jurisdictional boundaries of King—not Pierce—County.

From the beginning, both the Northern Pacific and Tacomans viewed the reservation as a barrier to economic development that had to be removed. Indeed, even before the bay became a terminus, the railroad unsuccessfully tried to remove the Puyallup people from their traditional home to an alien one on the Tulalip Reservation north of Seattle. The opportunity to gain access finally arose in 1887, when Congress authorized the elimination of all reservations nationwide through the allotment of land parcels to individual Native Americans. By the beginning of the

20th century and through a process that represents a low point in the city's history, Tacomans owned most of the former reservation land. With the successful northward shift of the boundary between Pierce and King County, the Puyallup River delta was now ready for its transformation into a port-industrial area.

While the delta remained a reserve, the Northern Pacific proceeded to create its commercial hub along the south shore of Commencement Bay, one that would ultimately create a waterway out of the various tendrils of the Puyallup. There, along the City Waterway, the railroad company greeted other private property owners, establishing New Tacoma's first industries within the tidelands south of the river. From 1888, when the St. Paul and Tacoma Lumber Company began operations on "The Boot," the future of Tacoma's waterfront consumed the attention of the entire city. Questions then arose about how to fund a collection of ideas, each one designed to create a port that would rival those in New York or Brooklyn.

As events unfolded, lines were drawn between Tacomans wanting every inch of Commencement Bay publicly owned by the city and those who remained convinced that only the private sector could develop a first-class port. After it became clear that private investors were not knocking on the city's door, local boosters grasped the port development opportunities made available by the Washington State legislature. One allowed property owners to create "waterway districts." The other allowed voters to approve the establishment of public "port districts." Tacomans used both possibilities.

This history combines both geography and chronology to explain the evolutionary development of Tacoma's waterfront. The essence of the story is found in chapters two through five, where the reader first travels along the shoreline from the Northern Pacific Railroad wharves into the City Waterway. Since the private development of the Hylebos began before the creation of the Port of Tacoma, its history is covered next, followed by a discussion of the port itself. (A question about nomenclature might arise over the use of the City Waterway and the Eleventh Street Bridge rather than the Thea Foss and the Murray Morgan Bridge. Justification rests in the reality that those living through the events portrayed here knew the places by their original names.)

Commencement Bay is more than the creation of the port-industrial area, so chapter six introduces the reader to both Browns Point and Point Defiance, along with the Tacoma Smelter and the town of Ruston. All of these features deserve histories of their own. Maritime and industrial workers, the focus of the afterword, in addition to periodic treatment throughout the history, also deserve more attention.

From point to point, Tacoma's waterfront is a living symbol of the city's commercial and industrial past, one that provided the economic base underlying the City of Destiny. This history provides only a few brush strokes of a much larger portrait. The authors hope that others will pick up the brush to continue and complete the work.

One

THE SETTING

In the spring of 1792, England's George Vancouver entered what he named Puget Sound as a part of his quest to find the Northwest Passage. During this voyage, he recorded abandoned villages and met Native Americans who displayed the characteristic scars of smallpox. Clearly white man's diseases had arrived before the first inland traders. Vancouver joined some of the survivors for a salmon lunch on a sandy beach now known as Browns Point and asked the locals about the large body of water that seemed to extend to the foothills of the mountain Vancouver named Mount Rainier. One native held up a hand indicating that it was a bay with many inlets. Not trusting the Native American's intelligence, the Englishman explored the bay, determined to his satisfaction that it was not the Northwest Passage, and sailed away. Vancouver was so uninterested in the body of water that he left it without a European name or did not sketch it. John Sykes drew this mountain view from Admiralty Inlet.

Charles Wilkes and his crew were the first Americans to explore Puget Sound, and it was because of his efforts that the region became part of the United States. He arrived here in 1841, established an observation post overlooking Puget Sound, and sent his crews inland to explore land not seen by Americans since Lewis and Clark's brief visit in 1805.

Wilkes also named geographical features neglected by George Vancouver, places such as Anderson and McNeil Islands, and Point Defiance. Even more importantly, he named Commencement Bay. This body of water that has been so crucial to Tacoma's history was where Wilkes started his survey of the Pacific Northwest. Commencement Bay is pictured in the upper right of this map.

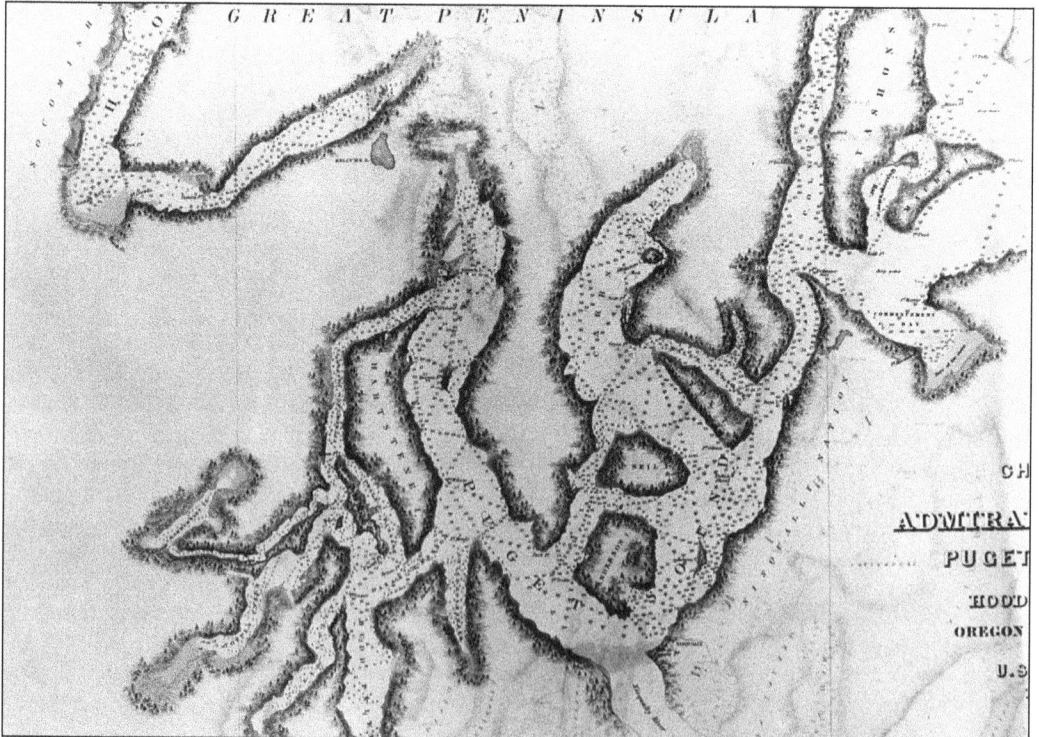

SALMON FISHERY ON CHICKELIS RIVER.

Wilkes, like explorers before him, was inclined to view the Native Americans as a part of the wilderness rather than a people with a distinct culture. Around Commencement Bay, the Puyallup Indians lived near ancient fisheries and hunting grounds. Every river and stream had sites for villages at locations so advantageous that American settlers recycled them into towns and cities. Wilkes did however document significant aspects of Native American life, including this view of early river fishing. The sketch depicts Native Americans on the Chehalis River south of Pierce County, but the Puyallup Indians probably used the same fishing techniques upstream from the Commencement Bay delta. Early maps show their salmon fishing locations in the bay, and ethnologists have identified village sites in what is now Tacoma's central business district. Sacred and burial sites existed where today's I-705 meets Schuster Parkway. The future site of the Tacoma Smelter was also a Native American burial site.

11

By 1853, Washington was a territory, and a new county named to honor Pres. Franklin Pierce had been formed with Commencement Bay its northern boundary. Congress appointed Isaac I. Stevens both territorial governor and superintendent of Indian affairs. He was also to lead a survey expedition to locate a possible northern route for a transcontinental railroad. Like the explorers who came before, Stevens had his artists along to portray the landscape, in this case a view of Mount Rainier from Whidbey Island. Stevens was also to establish treaties with the Native Americans and to create federal reserves where the Indians would live and be taught the American way of life. There were wars, massacres, and lynchings because of Stevens's treaties, with some tribes unwilling to "sign" and others dissatisfied over reservation land that deprived them of their cultural heritage. The Puyallup Tribe was able to renegotiate its treaty to create a reservation that included Commencement Bay land within the delta and along the north shore.

The treaties allowed the Puyallup Indians to use their historic fishing places located outside reservation land, and it was not uncommon to find canoes and native fishermen gathered along Tacoma's waterfront during the early years. The site for this 1890 photograph is unknown, although it might be the shoreline near present-day Fifteenth Street, a known location for a major Puyallup Indian village.

Native American gatherings along the Tacoma shoreline continued for years following the city's founding, always serving as a reminder as to who was here first. Early Tacoma photographer Arthur French captured this unique combination of past and present sometime during the latter years of the 19th century. Ladies and Native Americans pose by the Northern Pacific Railroad tracks. Perched atop the wooded bank is the Tacoma Hotel, completed in 1884.

Reservation headquarters were an early presence within the Tacoma landscape, as this 1894 Albert C. Carpenter photograph documents. The railroad tracks skirting the settlement led to the eastern Pierce County coal fields, in addition to meeting lines both crossing the Cascades and leading to and from Seattle. The tribal cemetery, located to the left of the church steeple, remains and can be seen when traveling River Road into the Puyallup Valley.

The Puyallup Indians appeared amused to see one of Tacoma's few women photographers—Hattie King—taking this picture sometime in the 1880s. As with many other images made at this time, the native culture is captured within the context of the new American presence. Except for the railroad tracks, everything in this view is Native American, but not for long.

14

In the summer of 1873, the Northern Pacific Railroad Company selected the shoreline below this bluff as its Puget Sound terminus. The first train arrived by the end of the year. By 1874, enough land had been cleared for the beginnings of a town located along Pacific Avenue near Seventh Street.

TACOMA, TERMINUS OF THE NORTHERN PACIFIC
Lithograph after a drawing by E. S. Glover, 1878. From the Stokes Collection, New York Public Library.

E. S. Glover created this idealized view of Tacoma in 1878. While evidence of the Puyallup Indian Reservation is missing, the artist provided a relatively accurate sense of the townscape. The large structure in the center of this view is the first Northern Pacific headquarters building located at Ninth and Broadway Streets.

Ten years after Glover sketched his view, the United States Geological Survey (USGS) produced this map of Commencement Bay. The line running through the lower third of the map—at least to where it ends in the water—was the northern boundary of Pierce County, meaning that both the Puyallup Indian Reservation and over half of the Puyallup River delta and tidelands were really in King County. The boundary remained at this location until the early years of the 20th century, when Pierce County voters agreed to move it northward. Even so, a court order was required to convince King County to relinquish control. By 1888, the Northern Pacific engineers had begun to dredge the City Waterway just east of Tacoma's downtown. Also that year, the St. Paul and Tacoma Lumber Company would construct a mill near the waterway's mouth on an island called "The Boot." Years were to pass before the delta would be developed into a port.

Two

TERMINAL WHARVES

When in 1873 Northern Pacific Railroad officials announced the selection of Tacoma as the site for its terminus, they meant some two miles of waterfront along the south shore of Commencement Bay. Construction of a wharf, seen here in 1886, was needed to connect rail to ship. The Blackwell Hotel, pictured behind the warehouse buildings on the left, was the first in New Tacoma. Tracks separate it from the major terminal warehouse. The development was almost completely isolated from both Old Tacoma, located to its north, and New Tacoma slowing growing on the bluff to the south. Residents had to hazard narrow pathways to catch passenger steamers embarking from the terminus. There is little activity pictured in this view, perhaps because the region was emerging from a depression initiated when Northern Pacific president Henry Villard declared bankruptcy in 1884. He was a man unloved in Tacoma because he put all his effort into boosting Portland as the terminus. Charles Wright replaced Villard as president shortly before this photograph was taken, and Tacomans looked to the future with hope.

Construction of the terminal wharf required years of pile driving and fill. Although undated, this view shows the northern portion under construction. A log boom for the Hatch Mill can be seen just above the Blackwell Hotel. Timber from the mill was used to build the wharf. The building in the foreground was another freight warehouse.

By 1886, the new warehouse was completed, and the holding basin was further filled to accommodate even more warehouses. Hattie King took this photograph looking south toward the Puyallup River delta. Even though it looked quite tidy, the terminal dock will continue to grow for many years to come. The pile drier is a hint of things to come.

When Thomas Rutter saw the terminal wharf around 1888, he saw a slow-paced working waterfront. Sailing ships and steamers shared moorage while horses and trains shared the dock. Freight was piled on the dock waiting for longshoremen to load it on one of the ships, and men were scattered about watching and waiting for something to happen.

Because of its rapidly paced construction, a part of the terminal wharves collapsed in 1894. Managers of the railroad company viewed the devastation from the comfort of the Northern Pacific headquarters building located a short distance away. The collapse should not have been a surprise to engineers. Even today, the south shore of Commencement Bay falls victim to winter storms.

19

Commerce with Asia was an early hope of Tacomans, and it is ironic to note that at the same time the Chinese were forcibly expelled from the city in 1885, local businessmen were planning for the future import of Chinese tea. Shipments began arriving by the 1890s and were unloaded at a terminal wharf adjacent to the coal bunkers.

The importation of tea continued, as this photograph shows. The occasion for the image was the introduction of a new conveyor designed, in part, to eliminate the number of longshoremen needed for the job. Even so, technology was not so advanced on the waterfront to keep the longshoremen from using the traditional hand truck.

Creating a rail yard along the Commencement Bay shoreline proved a major challenge for Northern Pacific officials; one solved by filling in Half Moon bay. The effort began as early as 1873 and continued into the 1880s and 1890s. Jackson photographed the progress as of 1885, and the image captured a moment of time in Tacoma's early history just before major changes were to alter the landscape. New Tacoma sits on the bluff. This is what the town looked like when the Chinese were expelled. One reason for their forced departure was a fear that a "Chinatown" would arise on the vacant land pictured in the upper right of the photograph. The Puyallup River delta is in the distance. Within three years, a lumber mill would rise on the island at the river's mouth. Also in 1885, the Northern Pacific board authorized the construction of a railroad line crossing Stevens Pass in the Cascades.

All roads led north to the terminal wharves in this 1886 Thomas Rutter view. Homes of Tacoma's elite overlook the sluicing and filling of the Half Moon yard. Pilings in the bay marked both the tidelands and the area to be filled in the future to create the City Waterway. A freshly graded Pacific Avenue now links new Tacoma to the wharves.

Within two years, most of the Half Moon Bay had been filled; it was now waiting the placement of more rails. The Northern Pacific was in a hurry to complete its work. Once Washington became a state in 1889, the company would have to prove that it had substantially developed the shoreline and had a right to own the tidelands. Most of the development seen so far, in other words, was done on land that the railroad did not own until after 1889.

The Northern Pacific headquarters building still overlooks the Half Moon yards. To the left, low tide marked the extent of future railroad development and the next area to be filled. Tacomans hoped that as the railroad expanded its development, the company would provide the city some shoreline space for a municipal dock. Years would pass before the wish was fulfilled.

Designed by railroad engineer Charles B. Talbot in 1887 and completed around 1889, the Northern Pacific headquarters building symbolized the role the railroad played in Tacoma's origins and survival. So too did the Tacoma Hotel whose roofline is seen in this 1888 view. In the distance, on The Boot, the St. Paul and Tacoma Lumber Company is under construction.

As the Northern Pacific continued its sluicing and filling southward toward the future City Waterway, it also expanded its shoreline development northward toward Old Tacoma. The company's coal bunkers were situated adjacent to the terminal wharves, and it was from here that eastern Pierce County coal was exported. Later sources called the housing in the foreground Old Women's, or Widow's, Gulch, but at the unknown time this photograph was taken, Native Americans were its probable residents. Newspaper articles at the time reported that in the 1880s the railroad company was trying to evict Native Americans living along the shoreline. By 1910, however, when the gulch was cleared for the construction of Stadium Bowl, old women resided in the shacks and were sluiced out along with the trees. Remnants of the coal bunkers can still be seen when driving along Schuster Parkway below Stadium High School and Bowl.

Coal and timber were resource necessities for the railroads of the West—timber was required for rail ties, boxcars, trestles, and wharves, and coal was a major source for fuel and power. In Pierce County, thanks to the land grant received from Congress, along with some rather questionable land dealings, the Northern Pacific owned most of the land bordering the Cascade Mountain foothills. In the mid-1870s, coal was discovered in eastern Pierce County, and its mining led to the creation of numerous company towns owned by assorted lumber, railroad, and coal concerns. Most were located within the confines of the Carbon River watershed. All of this coal ultimately found its way to the Commencement Bay bunkers. That from Carbonado was shipped to San Francisco to fuel Leland Stanford's various enterprises. The Northern Pacific's main mine was located outside Wilkeson, Fairfax fueled Tacoma's smelter, and Southern European and Russian immigrants did all the work.

The companies owning the coal towns were not the only users of the resource. As seen in this 1889 Thomas Rutter photograph, the coal bunkers were also a fueling station for navy vessels. Here the man-of-war *Thetis* is coaling, acquiring its load from the train situated on the rail trestle.

From the perspective of Commencement Bay, Rutter also provided a ship's-eye view of the coal being loaded into the central hold of a ship. The hillside has been logged, perhaps to provide the timber to build the bunkers. A solitary house overlooks the operation on the bluff in Tacoma's North End.

COAL BUNKERS AT TACOMA

Northern Pacific expanded and redeveloped other portions of the Commencement Bay shoreline, as well as the coal bunkers. Even though the entire facility was expanded in anticipation of more exports, it is difficult to assess how the expansion affected the economic development of Tacoma. The benefits most likely went to the owners of the company towns and Northern Pacific rather than either Tacoma or the workers in the mines, where explosions and cave-ins were a normal part of life. Besides showing the new version of the coal bunkers, this undated view also documents the northern end of the new wharf construction that would ultimately stretch from here into the City Waterway. Visible behind the coal bunkers was the Commercial Dock, one of many that were a response to Eastern Washington wheat arriving over the Cascade Division of the railroad.

With wheat, could there not be flour milling, asked both Tacomans and the Northern Pacific. As early as 1883, newspapers were reporting the immediate arrival of equipment to construct a proposed mill on the City Waterway. By 1888 and 1889, the Northern Pacific had leased some of its land located along Commencement Bay to the Puget Sound Flouring Mill. Elevator A, often seen in views of the shoreline, became the beginnings of a flour industry that marked the northern end of the railroad company's development. Near Elevator A was what Tacoma old-timers knew as Sperry Ocean Dock, a facility first constructed as a wheat warehouse. In this undated view, longshoremen are loading either wheat or flour onto a steam ship using hand trucks to cart the produce to a conveyor. Tea is loaded in the same manner. Sailing ships crowd Commencement Bay.

It is hard to imagine Tacomans in the middle of a drought in winter, but that is exactly what happened in 1929. There was not enough rain to provide the water to fuel the city's hydroelectric dams, even though earlier that year Cushman dam, located in Mason County, was dedicated. This facility, Tacomans assumed, would provide unlimited electric power far into the future. Instead, the city was faced with the possibility of blackouts just when people needed power the most. Tacoma petitioned the Navy Department to use the USS *Lexington* as a power source, and on December 15, 1929, the aircraft carrier tied up to the Baker Dock located near the coal bunkers and hooked a line to the city's power grid. To show their gratitude during the time the ship was in port, Tacomans entertained officers and crew whenever they had a chance and mourned the loss of the ship and its men in the Battle of Coral Sea in 1942.

The Baker Dock also witnessed tragedy. In February 1931, the driver of this Pacific Storage and Transfer truck lost his life, most likely when hit by a train. The shoreline had undergone substantial change by the time of the photograph. By 1914, the Northern Pacific had rerouted its main line so that it skirted Commencement Bay before entering the Point Defiance tunnel. (This is the route still used today.) By 1931, the coal bunkers were gone, although part of them can still be seen on the hillside. They became the victim of changing technologies and the shift to oil. The roadway to the left, with time, would become Schuster Parkway. Also seen on the left are the results of a Stadium Bowl slide, an occurrence that continuously plagued the facility. Baker Dock remained a fixture along the shoreline until destroyed by fire in the mid-1970s.

The Oriental (later the Baker) Dock marked the northern end of the original terminal wharf development, and Northern Pacific officials had plans for a magnificent hotel that would overlook the wharves. Bankruptcy in 1893 put an end to their dreams. The uncompleted shell sat neglected and suffered fire before architect Frederick Heath convinced the school board that it could be completed as a high school. The first class graduated in 1907.

Elevator A anchored the far end of a wharf complex that ended close to the Half Moon yard, where in this undated view the once-long wharf was undergoing dismemberment. Changing technologies and historical events were the reasons for the loss as the railroad's shoreline development accommodated itself to both the automobile and the emerging port located on the Puyallup River delta.

One major example of change was the completion of the Dock Street Bridge in the 1920s, representing another benchmark in the city's history. By crossing over the Half Moon yard, it linked automobile traffic on the City Waterway to the south shore of Commencement Bay. As the Port of Tacoma assumed greater importance, the railroad's original development was gradually abandoned until today there is only a modern grain terminal situated on land seen in the upper left of this photograph.

While the Half Moon yard and wharves dominated this undated view, the camera was pointed south toward Tacoma's new economic future on the City Waterway and Puyallup delta. Here the Northern Pacific Railroad controlled less of the land, and other developers, along with the City of Tacoma, played a greater role in determining what was to happen.

Three

THE CITY WATERWAY

The early waterfront history of the Puyallup River delta is a difficult one to tell; its ecology was part of the reason. Silting was and is a constant problem, one that without human intervention prohibited the delta's use for commercial and industrial purposes. Flooding too was a constant worry and required a complex rearrangement of upland rivers, along with dike construction, to tame the restless Puyallup. This kind of engineering took money, with much time and effort going into determining who should pay for the effort. Over time, Tacomans experimented with a variety of both public and private options. Troubling too were issues of property ownership and governmental authority. This undated photograph by Arthur French shows land owned by the federal government and tidelands owned by the state until purchased by private individuals. Besides these two jurisdictions, King County ruled the land pictured on the far left. Pierce County and the City of Tacoma governed the property on the right.

Tacoma boosted its settlement through this highly idealized bird's-eye view. And while the town was not as large as seen in this 1885 drawing, the artist was able to capture significant elements of the shoreline. By this time, the Northern Pacific construction and repair shops, seen just above the rail line, had been moved here from Kalama and were now a part of the urban landscape. The delta is poised for its first phase of dredging and filling.

Isaac Davidson photographed what the town really looked like in 1885. The Tacoma Hotel, located at the end of Ninth Street, was new. The only shoreline access was via the stairs seen on the left. There was not much to observe once navigating them downward, apart from the silted mudflats on the delta and the railroad tracks.

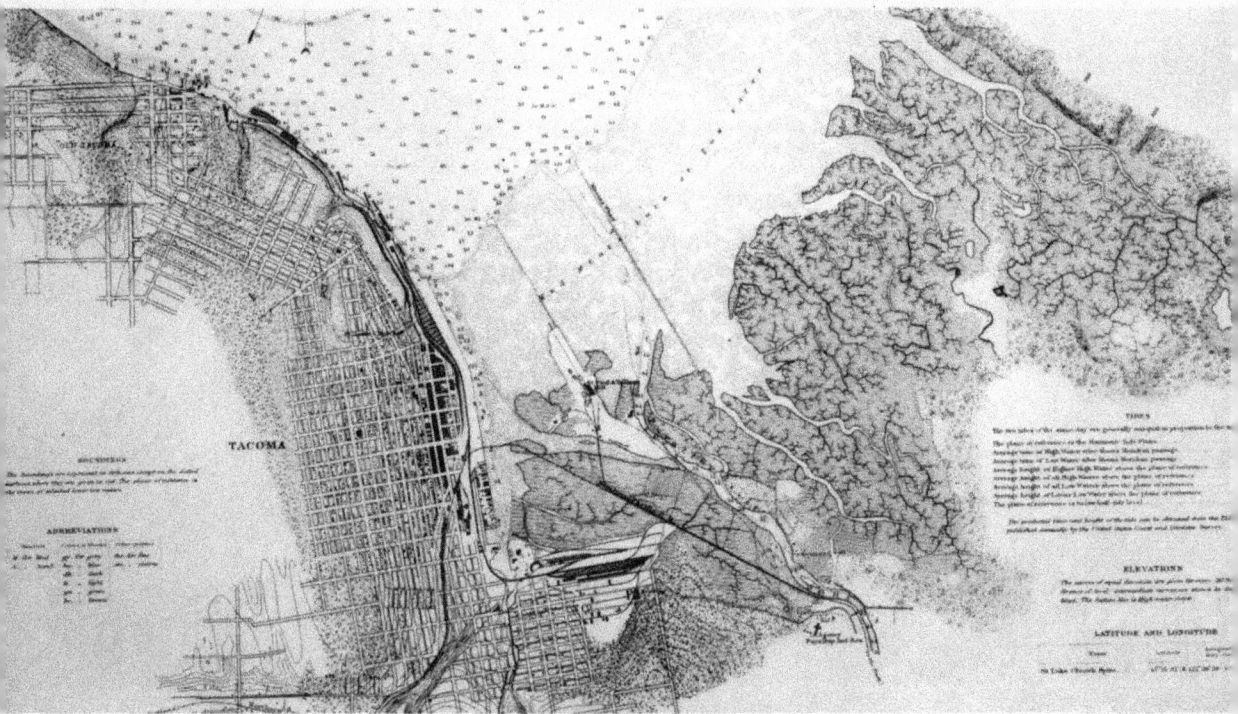

Commencement Bay—1899.

By 1899, the Commencement Bay shoreline had undergone significant changes. The City Waterway was now complete, with the Northern Pacific responsible for its engineering. The phased development began by damming the southern arm of the Puyallup, creating the Wheeler-Osgood Waterway, which was named for the lumber mill built on the site. The railroad also began to dredge and fill the tidelands northward toward the Half Moon yards. Tacomans watched this development with both trepidation and hope. The Northern Pacific's plans for the City Waterway provided no shoreline access to and from the city. In the 1890s, in the hope of acquiring some access, the city petitioned the Army Corps of Engineers to complete the dredging. The corps refused, arguing that the project would only benefit private property owners and not the public. Congress disagreed and ordered the corps to complete the dredging begun by the railroad. The work was completed by 1905, but Tacoma still had to wait a few more years before the Northern Pacific would grant public access to its City Waterway.

Much of the land formed by the dredging and filling to create the City Waterway was owned and controlled by the Northern Pacific. This undated photograph shows how the east shoreline appeared just before the construction of a linear complex of wheat and jobber warehouses. By 1901, when the work was done, there would be an uninterrupted line of buildings both occupying this site and filling the shoreline between here and the terminal wharves seen in the distance. The photographer stood on Tacoma's first Eleventh Street Bridge, a project approved by voters in the 1890s. Trains were running on the tracks toward the terminal wharves while on the bluff above the Tacoma Hotel has been expanded. Tacoma's fire department headquarters building, also constructed in the 1890s, is located north of the hotel.

Later another unknown photographer stood on the same bridge, this time to show sailing vessels tied to the wharf of G. W. McNear and Son's warehouse. (At least this company occupied the space in 1901.) Once completed, Kerr, Gifford, and Company would be the first occupant in the warehouse located to the north.

The city finally obtained its link to the City Waterway in 1911 when a part of the McNear warehouse became the Municipal Dock. It was a hard fought battle that included one unsuccessful 1890s attempt by the Tacoma Council to get a bill passed in the state legislature transferring ownership of all the shoreline to the city.

There was now a city port for the "Mosquito Fleet," the numerable steamers that carried passengers and freight to and from Puget Sound's various communities. Before this time, the fleet landed at assorted places, including the McCarver Street dock in Old Tacoma and the Northern Pacific's terminal wharf. The steamer *Indianapolis* is seen in this photograph.

People were now a vibrant part of the Tacoma waterfront, a phenomenon noticeably absent in many shoreline views. In this early version of mass transportation, the sounds and smells of all this humanity can only be imagined. One steamer was crammed with passengers, and more are on the dock perhaps waiting to take another one churning in the waterway.

Getting to and from the municipal dock from the city proved to be something of a challenge. Passenger bridges were the solution, and this photograph shows two leading to the wharves, warehouses, and the ground below. The one pictured in the distance led pedestrians down a steep set of stairs situated roughly at Eighth Street between the fire station and the Tacoma Hotel. The other was an adjunct to the Tacoma Hotel at Tenth Street and appears to be far more user friendly with its covered and gently sloping walkway. It is possible that the distant walkway was a route taken by passengers using the streetcar hub at Ninth and Broadway Streets who also needed to walk the distance to the Municipal Dock. Looking north toward the terminal wharves, the substantial changes undertaken by the Northern Pacific since 1901 are seen. Dock Street is absent in the view since automobiles and trucks have yet to appear. The complex of tracks was now the main line leading north to the Point Defiance tunnel.

When the second Eleventh Street Bridge was completed in 1913, an auxiliary walkway was provided to connect it to the Tacoma Municipal Dock. Originally the bridge was for streetcars and, when combined with the passenger steamers, symbolized the first phase of suburbanization in the city. Workers no longer had to live in the downtown area and walk to work either in the developing Puyallup delta, City Waterway, or shoreline wharves. Families could live some distance from work in a kinder environment away from the industrial smog. The bread winners could use cheap forms of mass transportation to their place of employment. The pedestrian walkway leading from the Tacoma Hotel is seen in the foreground of this view. Signs on the roof advertise trips to Seattle, while the Western States Grocery Company sign is a reminder that passenger ferry service shared the space with other businesses.

This undated photograph (and the one below) documented change along the waterway before the new dock and bridge. While the warehouses were in place, the old Eleventh Street Bridge, seen in the distance, still existed. Sailing ships share the waters with a passenger ferry probably heading to the terminal wharves, since there was no Municipal Dock yet.

Newer technologies were constantly changing the appearance of the waterfront. At the Shaffer Dock, cranes unload and load shipments on modern freighters. Trucks were now a feature on the dock. What remained constant were the trains hauling cargo, and trains continue to perform this role to the present day.

Over the years, Tacoma has had many mottos to boost its image. The most enduring was the "City of Destiny." At the city's beginnings, a poem accompanied this moniker: "Seattle! Seattle!/ Death Rattle! Death Rattle/ Tacoma! Tacoma!/ Aroma! Aroma!," with the aroma being the sweet smell of success. Later on, the mottos were more descriptive. Tacoma was the "lumber capital of the world," said one, and another was that Tacoma had the "longest wheat warehouse in the world." While something of an exaggeration, this undated photograph lends some support to the boosters' latter claim. Pictured here is the interior of one of the waterway's several warehouses, unfortunately unidentified in the image. It does, however, document the expansive interior of what was usually seen from the outside. The timbers used to build the warehouse were undoubtedly produced in one of the local mills. Few workers are pictured in this view; only four men load a truck. Perhaps this was all the workforce needed to load and unload the produce. Perhaps it is all the photographer wanted to show.

In 1901, this was the Kerr, Gifford, and Company warehouse. By the mid-1930s, the Waterside Milling Company used the building. Fire proved the major destroyer of the warehouse group; it was hard for the firefighters to get to the shoreline. The building was located just north of the Municipal Dock and right below the fire station.

Warehouse fires had to be fought primarily from the water using tugs and, in this case, Tacoma's new Fireboat No. 1 seen on the right. Constructed in 1929, the boat saw over 50 years of service before its retirement. The Tacoma Hotel ruins can be seen above the milling company fire. This building was destroyed by fire in 1935 even though a fire station was next door.

Ron Karabaich took this photograph from the Eleventh Street Bridge in the mid-1970s before the construction of I-705. The Municipal Dock is now a forlorn shell of its former self. It would continue to deteriorate until demolished by the city. North of the Municipal Dock are the ruins of the Waterside Milling Company fire. Recreation uses have replaced commercial ones on the City Waterway. Gradually more marinas will find their way to this shoreline. The distant warehouses have survived the test of time and presently host a maritime museum and retail/professional office spaces. Above the shoreline is vacant land once covered by the Tacoma Hotel and fire station. Both sites are waiting the completion of the new freeway before their development into the Frank Russell building and the replacement of what used to be called "Pretty Little Firemen's Park."

When historically venturing back in time along the City Waterway, Thea Foss was one of the first entrepreneurs found south of the Eleventh Street Bridge. She began with boat rentals, pictured here in 1890, before the business expanded to include the tugboats so familiar today. In the image below, the Foss Launch Company is seen to the left of the ship.

The British barkentine *Success* was originally a prison ship, one that would take felons and political radicals from Great Britain to Australia, just like earlier versions transported malcontents to the colonies before and after the Revolutionary War. *Success* became an early tourist attraction, visiting Tacoma in 1915, and somehow survived until 1946, when it burned to the waterline while anchored in Lake Erie.

45

In contrast to the west shore of the waterway north of the Eleventh Street Bridge, that portion near the Fifteenth Street Bridge has always been a hodgepodge of ever-changing development. This undated photograph features Tacoma's steam plant, a facility that in the early years powered many buildings in the central business district.

The Fifteenth Street Bridge could be the location for dramatic moments. In 1941, a car driven by a Mrs. Woodward toppled off the structure. Accidents of this nature were common as drivers learned to maneuver over bridges originally not designed for the automobile. Whether Mrs. Woodward survived is not known.

Beginning in the late 1880s, when the Lister family established its foundry, the southern parts of Tacoma along the waterway were the city's first industrial zone. Lumber and flour mills were also present early on. This ship is anchored near the end of the waterway adjacent to the former location of the Northern Pacific shops.

The Tacoma Gas Plant is seen in the distance of the above photograph. In 1883, J. W. Sprague, Robert Wingate, and J. H. Houghton organized the Tacoma Gas and Light Company. The plant, located near Twenty-third and A Streets, produced the first light for city residents, businesses, and streets.

Sometimes it takes a more modern view to explain the past. In the early years, before a depot was constructed near this intersection, both passenger and freight trains whizzed through the Seventeenth Street and Pacific Avenue crossing, stopping only after reaching the terminal wharves. It took more than a century for the railroad to abandon the route. (Fredrickson photograph.)

In 1971, Fredrickson captured the complex of rails located east of the Union Station. Before moving to South Tacoma in the 1890s, the Northern Pacific shops were located here. Businesses located along the waterway are seen on the left, with Albers Mill the fuzzy building in the distance. In less than a generation, all but Albers and the Union Station would disappear to make way for a freeway.

Before engineers began creating the City Waterway, streams from Galliher's Gulch entered Commencement Bay. It was here that Nicholas DeLin established his sawmill in 1852, only to abandon it following the outbreak of war with the Native Americans. It was also near here that the Indian Henry Trail led to a Puyallup Indian village. In 1896, the gulch was home to what was then called the "longest and only exclusive bicycle bridge in the world." Credit for its construction goes to E. G. Dorr, L. G. Jackson, George Sheeder, and W. E. Newton who, besides spearheading construction of the bridge, also oversaw the creation of some 30 miles of bicycle paths throughout the city. The more than 5,000 bicycle riders were taxed $1 each to fund the project. The bridge, dismantled in the 1930s to make way for filling the gulch, was located near Lincoln High School. This undated photograph provides an opportunity to imagine what early settlers saw at the end of the City Waterway.

By 1927, development on the east side of the waterway between the Eleventh and Fifteenth Street bridges was entering a new phase. The Wheeler Waterway, seen in the center of this photograph, was once a Puyallup River channel. The Petrich family's boat works is seen on the left. Behind the twin stacks of the city steam plant, a railroad bridge carries trains into the undeveloped port-industrial area.

The railroad infrastructure was clearly in place by 1927. Union Pacific tracks crossed the Fifteenth Street Bridge and ended east of the waterway. The Northern Pacific freight yards and roundhouse are seen in the distance along with the Hawthorne industrial area. Italian immigrants dominated the residential neighborhood located there.

Early development on the east side was dependent on the railroad, and until after the turn of the 20th century, the Northern Pacific alone determined when and where tracks were to go. It took a Supreme Court decision in 1904 to break the monopoly, thus allowing the entry of additional lines. The Fifteenth Street Bridge, pictured in this undated view, and the arrival of the Union Pacific in 1910, symbolized the change.

Passengers arriving or leaving from the Municipal Dock in 1927 would see this development across the City Waterway. P. J. Fransioli and Company warehoused hay, grain, and feed along with the bags needed to cart the produce away. Soon an oil storage and refining facility would emerge on the vacant land to the left.

Joe M. Martinac started building boats on the City Waterway in 1924 after learning the trade in both Gig Harbor at Skansies and Old Tacoma with the Barbare brothers. Through the years of building tuna seiners, traditions emerged within the Martinac firm. When workers placed the last plank into a wood hull, for example, they would pause to celebrate, as pictured above. Pictured here in 1947 Roberts photograph, from left to right, Red MacFarlane, Norval Keck, Charlie Kristovich, unknown, and George "The Legend" Nichols honor the ritual. When Martinac shifted to steel hulls this tradition ended. The Royal Pacific, left, was one of the last wood-hull seiners.

11TH ST. BRIDGE TACOMA WN.

Early Tacomans were quite willing to tax themselves to fund improvements viewed as public necessities. Voters agreed to establish publicly owned power and water facilities in the 1890s, for example. Twice residents agreed that a bridge linking downtown Tacoma and the east side of the City Waterway was an absolute necessity. The significance of this decision cannot be stressed enough, for in many ways it was an act of defiance against the Northern Pacific Railroad. When voters funded the first bridge in the 1890s, there was no easy way for workers who walked to work to get from their homes in Tacoma to the new industries then located on the east side of the waterway. Since none of the new developments directly benefited the railroad company, however, officials saw no reason to provide the access. Voting for a new bridge in 1911 indicated changes in transportation and bridge construction technologies. Workers might still cross the bridge on foot, but they could also take a streetcar, bus, or drive their own automobiles.

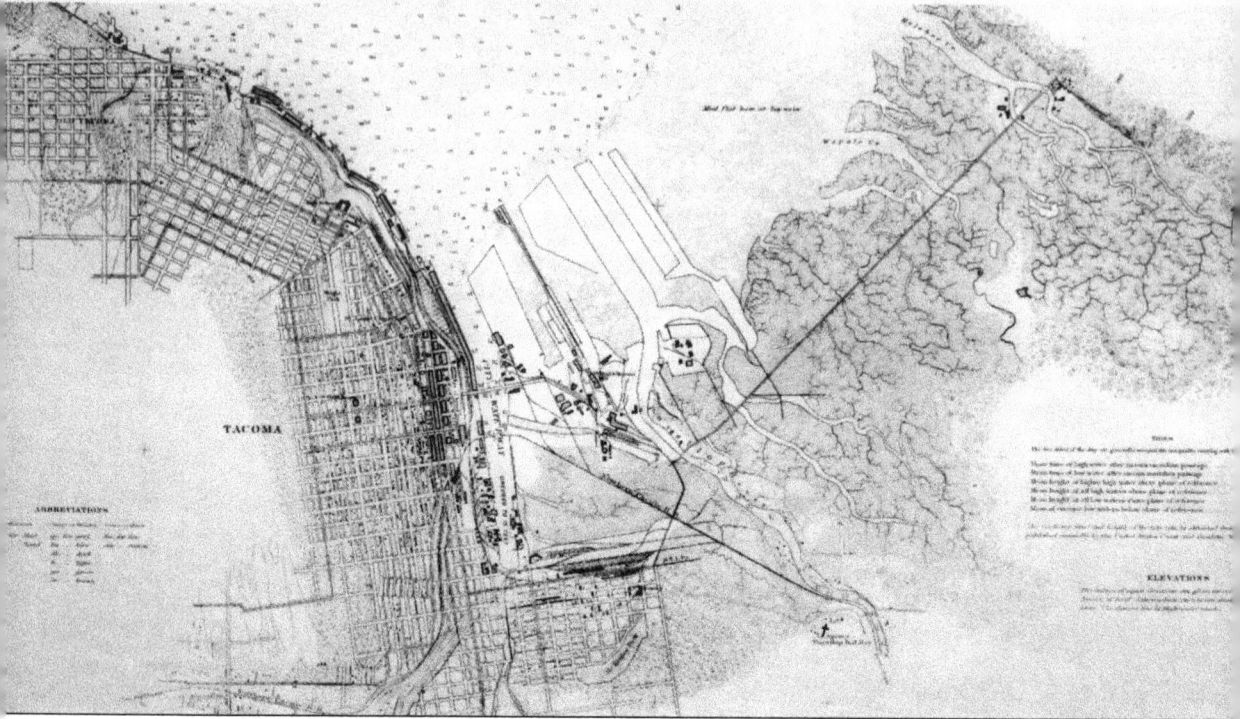

By 1910, USGS mapmakers would show a new shoreline along Commencement Bay. The Eleventh Street Bridge crossed the completed City Waterway and led to the St. Paul and Tacoma Lumber Company mill, originally built on The Boot. New wharves extended out into the tidelands around the mouth of the Puyallup River. But the changed geographical and man-made features do not tell the whole story of what had happened by this time. No longer is the delta under the collective control of the Puyallup Tribe of Indians. Beginning in 1887, the Native Americans were allotted portions of the reserve that each would own outright in 1904. Even before that time, however, a consortium of Tacoma businessmen and real estate developers, who negotiated questionable contracts with each individual Native American property holder, controlled most of the land. In 1906, the Puyallups responded by unsuccessfully suing James Ashton, along with other members of the group, in the hopes of retaining ownership of the tidelands fronting the former reservation. It was not until the 1990s that the tribe acquired compensation for what was clearly an injustice.

Four

THE HYLEBOS

After 1903, when the Puyallup Reservation theoretically ceased to exist, owners along Hylebos Creek were faced with the question of how to pay for the creation of a privately owned port-industrial waterway comparable to the one located adjacent to the city. Since the creek was not navigable, obtaining immediate assistance from the Army Corps of Engineers was impossible. And unlike the City Waterway where the Northern Pacific was the major owner, there were many owners to accommodate on the Hylebos. The answer came via a Washington State Legislative measure allowing for the creation of private development districts funded by the property owners taxing themselves. The (Hylebos) Commercial Waterway District No. 1 was established in 1914, and dredging began. Named to honor the Roman Catholic mission priest Fr. Peter Francis Hylebos, the waterway and delta beyond appears almost idyllic in this Richards Photo Studio view taken from Northeast Tacoma in 1942. Little is pictured to suggest that the waterway had begun to take shape almost 30 years before or that development was underway before Pierce County voters agreed to create the Port of Tacoma in 1918.

One of the challenges in creating the Hylebos Waterway District was ownership of the tidelands, or the undeveloped mudflats pictured here. Three men—James Ashton, Allen C. Mason, and Frank C. Ross—owned most of this property and had plans to create their own private port facility, one that would stretch from the Hylebos to the Puyallup River. Indeed, in plans published in the *Tacoma Daily News* in 1907, the trio proposed a Hylebos Waterway that would extend a mile eastward and then ultimately connect to the Puyallup River. This would have rerouted the river's mouth into the Hylebos. Unnamed "eastern capitalists" were to fund the project. The plan never materialized, in part because its proponents were unable to interest potential investors but also because of local hostility against the developers. At the same time Ashton, Mason, and Ross were publicizing their intentions, the Washington State Legislature was passing a bill that would allow counties to create public port districts. In the debate that followed, it became clear that most Tacomans preferred public to private development on the Puyallup delta.

56

Taken in 1963, this Richards Studio photograph provides a view of the turning basin under construction via the channelization of Hylebos Creek. The Port of Tacoma ordered the aerial perspective to show the quantity of land available for industrial development. Parts of the town of Fife are pictured in the foreground.

Unlike today, in 1955, the mouth of the waterway was wider with an irregularly filled shoreline to the north. At this time, the south side of the Hylebos and the north side of Blair Waterway west of Eleventh Street was home to a U.S. Navy station and mothballed fleet. The piers seen in the lower right no longer exist. (Photograph by Richards Studio.)

This choice waterfront industrial site is the largest available in the heart of the busy Tacoma Industrial Area today.

In the undated aerial photograph above, the north shore of the Hylebos is now filled. The turning basin is seen in the distance, and storage tanks dominate the upper left of the waterway. While the Naval Reserve still occupies the south side, the mothballed fleet is gone. The Puyallup River channel (seen on the right) extends eastward into the valley. Gradually the Hylebos acquired its fair share of industries, especially boatbuilders and chemical processing plants. But in the undated aerial view below looking south, land is available for more. The marshy lakes will become the Blair Waterway.

Taylor Way

Hylebos Waterway

In the early years of the 20th century, railroad tracks—later an extension of Eleventh Street—ran from the City Waterway to the Hylebos. The first bridge to cross the creek was a wooden drawbridge, one replaced in 1925 by this 800-ton lift span. Photographer Marvin Boland caught the bridge tender either raising or lowering the bridge in January 1926, when it was only three months old. According to newspaper accounts, the structure "was the only bascule type bridge in Pierce County" at the time. The new bridge was a momentous occasion, one tied to a citywide effort to improve shoreline access. In addition, residents living in Northeast Tacoma would now have a more direct route to downtown. At this time, most of those living on the north side of Commencement Bay traveled to and from Tacoma by boat.

An abandoned lumber mill dominated this 1930 Richards photograph of the Hylebos Bridge and waterway. Tacoma's new steam plant is seen in the lower left. The southern shore of the waterway is ripe for development, with only the Hooker Chemical plant occupying the space. Property owners felt that a deeper channel was needed before additional industries would locate here.

In 1931, the Army Corps of Engineers agreed to dredge the channel, but only if a new bridge with greater clearance was constructed. When a new bridge had yet to appear by 1935, the federal government condemned the old crossing, inspiring work to begin. Richards documented the result in May 1939 shortly after its completion.

Shipbuilding was one of the first industries along the Hylebos, beginning in 1918 when Old Tacoma's Barbare brothers moved their yard to the new waterway. There they joined the Todd Dry Dock and Construction Company, constructing ships for America's World War I navy, and Congress established the Emergency Fleet Corporation to oversee the project. By 1918, when the ship pictured here under construction was completed, the war was over. (Photograph by Richards Studio.)

On November 30, 1918, Todd shipyard workers gathered before the ship launching. The war was over by this time, and the Emergency Fleet Corporation had no reason to fund any more ships. The result was economically devastating for the Puget Sound economy. Early in 1919, workers in both Tacoma and Seattle called for a general strike. Tacoma's strike—called a Bolshevist plot by local newspapers—lasted three days.

Western Boat Building, owned by the Petrich family, was another Old Tacoma concern that ultimately found its way to the Hylebos. At first, the yard was relocated below the Eleventh Street Bridge, but when fire destroyed that facility, the company, in 1968, built anew on Marine View Drive. The enlarged plant allowed Western Boat to construct larger vessels and to undertake dockside repairs. (Photograph by Richards Studio.)

When the "YFB-87" hit the water on December 18, 1969, Western Boat witnessed this first launching at its new facility. The car and passenger ferry was modeled after the *Hiyu*, whose route took it between Point Defiance and Vashon Island. This boat, however, was not intended for Puget Sound waters. Instead it was towed to Pearl Harbor and used in runs to Ford Island.

Tacoma Boatbuilding was one of several local manufacturers of tuna seiners. Initially located on the Sitcum Waterway, the yard moved to the Hylebos in 1969. With land to spare, Tacoma Boatbuilding could more easily organize the boatbuilding process. The buildings closest to the hillside were construction sheds for aluminum and steel fabrication leading to the launching ways. The building nearest the water was reserved for pipefitters and electricians. Although a photograph is not readily available, Mike Kazulin was another Old Tacoma Croatian with a boatyard on the Hylebos. In the 1950s, he leased it to Joe M. Martinac, whose own yard on the City Waterway was running to full capacity. In 1951, the company had tuna seiners *Royal Pacific*, *Mona Lisa*, and *LuBrito* in various stages of completion at their main facility and a fourth ready to launch at Kazulin's. All the boats would ultimately join the tuna seine fishing fleet in Southern California. (Photograph by Richards Studio.)

While the new Tacoma Boatbuilding facility was under construction on the Hylebos, the firm continued its work at the Port Industrial Yard. Richards took this photograph on May 22, 1970, the day the *Captain Vincent Gann* was launched. The *Tacoma News Tribune* reported at the time that nine fishing boats had been launched at this location since 1966.

Mrs. Edmund Gann, wife of the ship's owner, broke the champagne bottle over the hull before the tuna seiner successfully slid into the water. Those who attended the launching look on as the boat was secured to the dock. The *Captain Vincent Gann* would be the last Tacoma Boatbuilding vessel launched from this location. It was most likely hauled to the Hylebos for its final fitting. (Photograph by Richards Studio.)

Lumber booms in the Hylebos were a constant reminder that lumber mills shared the Hylebos with boatbuilders. The Tidewater Mill was constructed in 1918 on land purchased from James Ashton. When Marvin Boland took this photograph in 1921, the mill was one of only a local few that could produce long construction beams.

Deepwater moorage allowed more than one vessel to load at the Tidewater Mill, and in 1926, Marvin Boland caught two tied up at the wharf. One was the *Cacique*, posed behind logs waiting for milling. The facility was located at the north end of Eleventh Street and, according to a 1918 *Tacoma Daily Ledger* article, exported three-fourths of its timber.

Following World War I, chemical-manufacturing plants found their way to the Hylebos. Hooker Electrochemical Company was the first to arrive in the 1920s, and it distinguished itself by creating a well-planned and architecturally interesting complex. The plant continued to operate into the latter years of the 20th century and received momentary notoriety in 2006, when the smoke stack was demolished. (Photograph by Richards Studio.)

In 1950, Hooker Chemical held its board of directors meeting in Tacoma. To celebrate the event, the men posed for a group portrait in front of one of their tank cars. John D. Rue, the plant manager, is in the first row (extreme left). Sales manager Albert Hooker is fifth from the left in the first row, while A. J. Rosengarth, plant superintendent, is on the far right. The remainder of the men are unidentified. (Photograph by Richards Studio.)

Pennsylvania Salt Manufacturing Company (later Pennwalt) selected this site on the Hylebos in 1929 because of the low electrical rates provided by public power and the availability of water, rail, and motor transportation. Its establishment also coincided with changes in the local forest industry where timber milling was replaced with pulp, paper, and plywood manufacturing. New forest products needed the new chemistry. (Photograph by Richards Studio.)

By the outbreak of World War II, aluminum plants were drawn to Tacoma, again because of inexpensive public power. In addition, the product was a necessary component when building airplanes. Kaiser Aluminum, located within view of the Hylebos, later expanded its operations to include a site on the Sitcum Waterway. Power from Grand Coolie Dam fueled the wartime plant. (Photograph by Richards Studio.)

Even though Pearl Harbor was not attacked until December 7, 1941, the United States had begun to mobilize for war in 1940 following the Nazi invasion of France. While federal war planners focused eastward across the Atlantic and Hitler, defensive measures in the Pacific Northwest remained meager and outdated. Pictured here is part of an exercise conducted on April 17, 1941. Hooker Chemical forms a backdrop for the 205th Coast Artillery unit. The men and their weapons were pointed toward Fort Lewis where Gray Field Army Air Corps planes were posed to simulate a nighttime attack on the Hylebos. Within a year, the scenario would be different. Surviving destroyers from Pearl Harbor would be sent to Bremerton's Puget Sound Naval Shipyard for retrofitting, while Tacoma's Port—and the Hylebos—expanded its industrial capacity to accommodate all that was required for fighting the war.

Five

FROM DELTA TO PORT

The Puyallup River begins via a glacier on Mount Rainier. Today, as it meanders out of the foothills, it meets the Carbon River and then the White River before following a diked channel to Commencement Bay. This was not the scenario when the settlement first began. Originally the free-flowing Puyallup regularly flooded, causing havoc for farmers and city dwellers alike. The White River originally ran northward joining the Green and Black Rivers to form the Duwamish at Seattle. Today's White River was then a small creek, sometimes called the Stuck, which would channel floods into Pierce, rather than King County. Taming the rivers was therefore a major preoccupation of Tacomans as the delta was reshaped into a port-industrial area. Such matters did not concern Arthur French as he captured this idyllic moment of mountain grandeur when the St. Paul and Tacoma Lumber Company was the city's first tidelands industry.

Both the St. Paul and Tacoma and Wheeler-Osgood mills were in operation when Thomas Rutter ventured to the Puyallup Indian Reservation around 1890. The building in the foreground was the Native American schoolhouse where youngsters learned the American way of life. Delta marshes separated the reservation from town.

Carleton Watkins wandered into the marsh for this c. 1882 photograph before there was a Tacoma Hotel, railroad headquarters building, or shops. The Lister ironworks formed the southern boundary of the town. Watkins provided one of the few available close-up views of the delta before its transformation into a port.

Railroad tracks were the first to cross the marsh and became the infrastructure for future development. The first line, seen here in an undated Levy photograph, took trains to the eastern Pierce County coal mines. By 1887, trains crossing Stampede Pass initially followed this route. While the photograph is undated, the appearance of the Tacoma Hotel indicates a post-1884 skyline.

By 1926, all of the transcontinental lines—including the Great Northern seen in the foreground— had arrived and railroad tracks crisscrossed the delta. Tacoma sported a more architecturally modern skyline overlooked by the stately Pierce County Courthouse. The marshes were still being prepared for industrial land, but out of view to the right, the Port of Tacoma's piers were underway. (Photograph by Chapin Bowen.)

Creating the Port of Tacoma in 1918 was a laborious process, involving years of debate over the "who's" of both funding and the ownership of the tidelands that had to be filled to build the piers. Without the dock facilities, there would be no industry, and without industry, Tacoma would die on the vine, or so local boosters concluded. When Tacoma began, private funds, with a little help from Congress, paid for the work of creating the City Waterway along with the expansion that took the wharves to the Puyallup River. But the cost of developing the remainder of the tidelands was beyond the means of local entrepreneurs. The Washington State Legislature solved the problem by letting counties create special taxing districts for port development, much as special districts fund schools. When Pierce County voters agreed to create a port district, Tacomans celebrated through yet another motto—"Watch Tacoma Grow." Little did the original port founders know that growth would be an ever-changing and lengthy process.

According to an early caption accompanying an 1891 photograph, an active debate was in progress regarding whether or not industries built on the Puyallup delta would sink into the mud. While that never happened, there was always a possibility that the floods would carry the businesses away. The problem intensified after 1906 when a log jam diverted the White River into the Puyallup, and King County farmers and engineers wanted to make the change permanent by constructing a concrete dam. Pierce County sued King County over the issue, and it was not until 1913 that the matter was resolved. Based on the testimony of Hiram Chittenden, then district engineer for the army, "nature had transferred the course" of the White River, "and it would be simpler to perpetuate it than to change it again." The dam stayed, but King County had to pay 60 percent of the costs for flood control. Upland improvements were made, but nothing was done to stop the flooding on the Puyallup River delta.

By 1933, King and Pierce Counties had spent more than $3 million on river improvements to control the rivers. In December of that year, however, massive flooding proved once again that the White and Puyallup Rivers had yet to be tamed. Floodwaters extended all the way to Commencement Bay and destroyed much of the work then underway to create and improve the port-industrial area. After years of petitioning Congress, federal funds had finally been authorized to improve the various waterways through additional dredging and diking. The Army Corps of Engineers had been working on the project for years when, as this 1933 aerial photograph shows, its work washed away. By this time, too local jurisdictions and businessmen had realized that solving the problem of flooding within the delta required taming the waters further upstream. In 1936, Congress allocated funds to the corps for the construction of Mud Mountain Dam on the White River. World War II delayed its completion until 1948.

District No.	Area-Acres	Assessment
1	905	$600.
2	907	250.
3	620	150.
4	569	100.
5	635	50.
6	1380	35.
7	487	25.
8	483	15.
9	2075	25.
10	1461	17.

**PROPOSED WAPATO-HYLEBOS
WATERWAY DISTRICT**
AND ASSESSMENT ZONES

— Scale —

L.A. Nicholson
Civil Engineer

From 1907, when James Ashton first publicized his plans for the Puyallup delta, Tacomans were awash with ideas as to how the various creeks could be developed into a port-industrial area. The chamber of commerce served as a clearinghouse for them and came up with a few of their own, most premised on the private ownership of the facilities. Civil engineer L. A. Nicholson produced this map sometime before 1918. Wapato Creek, rather than Hylebos, was the focal point of this development. The main waterway extended two miles southeast, while a branch led south to where Puyallup Avenue is today. A Wapato-Hylebos Waterway District would be formed to fund the project. All of the property owners are identified on the map, and the amount each would have been assessed was to be based on their proximity to the waterway. Tacoma Chamber of Commerce members were avid supporters of this plan until 1918, when they were persuaded to support a publicly owned port.

In 1888, in the largest, single private land deal in American history up to that time, the founders of the St. Paul and Tacoma Lumber Company purchased 90,000 acres of timberland—most in Pierce County—from the Northern Pacific. The railroad company, according to Murray Morgan, "also tried to sell" the founders "a mill site on the south side of Commencement Bay, out beyond Old Tacoma." Chauncy Griggs, Addison Foster, and Henry Hewitt Jr., however, opted for a site on The Boot, land closer to the Puyallup River and away from both Old and New Tacoma. The company was the first to locate within the future port-industrial area and ultimately became the largest exporters of milled timber. Its logging railroads wound their way into the forests of the county, and the harvesting of timber opened new areas for settlement. The mill's dock extended into Commencement Bay where ships gathered for loading. These freighters will take Pierce County timber to Australia, China, and Japan.

"Situated directly opposite the Tacoma Hotel, the mill is a prominent feature in the landscape, and is a handsome structure," reported boosters shortly after the mill opened. The ghosts of the mill remain, and Tacomans see them daily within the operations of Simpson Paper, whose acquisition followed a 1983 friendly takeover by Champion International.

The St. Regis paper mill was located next door to the St. Paul operations and, by 1947, had established a world market for its pulp and paper exports. Years later, the two firms merged under the St. Regis name. In 1966, Richards documented longshoremen loading the SS *Alemannia* with 500 tons of pulp headed to Bremen, Germany. (Photograph by Richards Studio.)

William C. Wheeler and George R. Osgood founded their lumber mill in 1889 and located near the St. Paul and Tacoma on the waterway that still bears the company name. The firm specialized in fir and cedar doors, sash, blinds, interior finish, and millwork, first for local building construction and then for export. The complex seen here was the first of several built on the same site as, over the years, fires consumed the plant. In the early years of the 20th century, Wheeler-Osgood introduced plywood—specifically the manufacture of doors—to the area's building industry, and by World War I, doors and other plywood products consumed the business. From this time forward, the company achieved national notoriety for its efforts to improve the plywood process in terms of both manufacturing and sales. The firm prospered into the 1950s when, in the words of a company historian, "the plant in Tacoma was showing its age." Rather than upgrade the facility, owners closed its doors in 1951.

In 1936, at the age of 31, Benjamin "Ben" Cheney located his stud mill in the port-industrial area, gradually expanding his operations to Medford, Oregon, along with Greenville, Pondosa, and Arcadia, California. Cheney loved baseball and sponsored teams in the towns where his mills were located. At one time, he was part owner of the San Francisco Giants. He is best known, however, for bringing professional baseball to Tacoma when, in 1960, the city had an opportunity to acquire a Pacific Coast League team. His contribution of money and San Francisco Seals seats and lights gave Tacoma the stadium that still bears his name. His generosity was made possible through the success of the Cheney Lumber Company pictured in this 1947 dockside view. Crane No. 2 stands ready to load stacks of studs onto a freighter tied to the wharf. (Photograph by Richards Studio.)

One port pier was filled with Cheney studs in 1947. The company was first established to manufacture 12-foot studs that were exported and then cut to size for railroad ties. Then the GI Bill led to a housing boom following World War II, one that produced a demand for eight-foot framing. By cutting the length of his studs, Cheney was able to fill the need. (Photograph by Richards.)

This 1947 photograph by Richards is something of a puzzle. Lumber handlers appear to be loading a freighter with Cheney studs. (This ship appears in other images in the series.) But what are the men really doing? It appears to be a strange way to load a freighter, so perhaps the men are planking the ship's deck.

The nature of Tacoma's lumber industry began to change long before to the outbreak of World War II. Trees remained in relative abundance, but the demand for milled timber had dropped, and companies began to look for alternative uses for the product. By 1948, longshoremen would be found loading bundled pulp onto freighters for export. (Photograph by Richards Studio.)

Exporting logs was another alternative after the war. Here lumber handlers load the freighter *Tahsis* with logs and milled timber. The scene shows an interesting contrast with workers unloading the log truck by hand in view of one of the port's dockside cranes, aided too by an automated system onboard the ship. (Photograph by Richards Studio.)

Not all ships to the port were freighters. On April 1, 1933, *Yukomo*, the flagship of the Imperial Japanese Fleet, along with the *Iwate*, arrived at the port piers for a three-day visit. While the 1,500 officers and crew went on leave, Tacomans toured the ships. In less than a decade, the United States and Japan would be at war. (Photograph by Marvin Boland.)

Within four years of the Japanese visit, ships from the U.S. Navy paid their respects during the 1937 Fleet Week. By that time, Japan had already invaded Manchuria and China and war clouds were forming in Europe. Tacomans were able to celebrate one more fleet week in 1938 before war broke out in Europe and America's navy prepared to enforce U.S neutrality. (Photograph by Richards Studio.)

Every city had a "Hooverville" during the Depression, which followed the 1929 stock market crash. Tacoma's was located on the delta. In 1943, the Tacoma Waterfront Defense Committee sponsored a drive to clean out the buildings with the Coast Guard doing the work. The project was inspired by the fear that the shacks would spark a major fire if enemy bombers attacked the city. (Photograph by Richards Studio.)

The cleanup also included the collection of debris both to prevent fires and to locate materials that could be recycled for the war effort. While the Coast Guard scoured Port of Tacoma land, other property owners were encouraged to do the same. The port-industrial area must have been a rather messy place to have been the subject of such a campaign. (Photograph by Richards Studio.)

The Port Industrial Bridge over the Blair Waterway opened in December 1953, five months before this photograph by Richards was taken. The bridge was not needed until then because the waterway did not extend east from Eleventh Street until after World War II. The camera is looking west where mothballed jeep carriers were stored following the Korean War.

The waterway, initially named for Wapato Creek, was dredged to Eleventh Street by 1930. At this time, USGS maps show only rails running through this part of the port area. Therefore, to some degree, the completion of the Blair Bridge with its concrete roadway marked a significant transportation shift in the port area. (Photograph by Richards Studio.)

Even though the Taylor Avenue plant now sits idle, Kaiser Aluminum had been a fixture in the port-industrial area since World War II. By the 1960s, this massive dome located near Pier 7 stored alumina imported from Australia. The dome shared the wharf with one of the Port of Tacoma's "new" 205-foot cranes. With the port's ability to now unload a freighter, a ship no longer had to carry its own loading and unloading equipment.

A conveyor carried alumina from the ship to the dome. Star Iron and Steel, a Tacoma industry, fabricated the equipment facing the Sitcum Waterway. This photograph (and the one at the top of the page) was taken by Richards in 1967, close to the time of the structure's construction. Shifts to container storage in the port-industrial area have removed the dome from the landscape.

On December 3, 1948, Rainier Steel Corporation became Tacoma's first plant of its type. Located on Lincoln Avenue between the Blair and Hylebos Waterways, the company recycled scrap iron in its manufacturing process. Times were ripe for this kind of operation, especially since people were beginning to get rid of their old prewar cars. This 1949 Richards aerial photograph was taken a month after the plant fired up.

On the first day of operations, Richards captured an interior view of the Rainier Steel Corporation blast furnace. President and company general manager Eugene Cunningham, wearing a top coat, hat, and sun glasses, is on the right. Phil E. Haglund, whose position with the company is unknown, joined him on the left.

The Pacific Iron and Steel Works fabricated logging and hoisting equipment, steel castings, and dredging machinery needed in many of Tacoma's wartime industries. The manufacturing complex, pictured here in 1943, was located on Canal Street, before the roadway's name was changed to Portland Avenue. (Photograph by Richards Studio.)

Joseph E. Landsburg, whose association with the Pacific Iron and Steel Works is unknown, commissioned this interior view of the manufacturing plant on December 11, 1945. World War II was now over, and maybe the company's usefulness was as well. There is the feeling of an era's technological end when looking at both the exterior and interior of the building. (Photograph by Richards Studio.)

Exporting grain from Eastern Washington was a continuing theme in Tacoma's history, but over time, the City Waterway's "longest wheat warehouse in the world" gave way to vertical concrete silos. The Washington Cooperative Farmers Association grain elevator and feed mill, located on Taylor Way between a boatbuilder and Buffelin Lumber Company, opened in March 1949.

Richards took both this image and the one pictured at the top of the page in 1948. The Port of Tacoma grain elevator was completed in 1940 and was managed until 1951 when operations were taken over by the Archer-Daniels-Midland Company. The photograph shows the conveyor system, which moved grain to ships that carried it to America's allies during the cold war.

These two views, taken in 1947 and 1967, illustrate how technology changed the work of longshoremen during the course of 20 years. In 1947, the *Tacoma Times* celebrated Labor Day by showing longshoremen hauling flour on hand trucks to a freighter whose cranes lift bundles onboard. By 1967, at the Kaiser Aluminum Pier 7 import facility, there is little need for many longshoremen. The port crane unloaded the alumina from the ship. It was then poured into a hopper and moved by a conveyor to storage. Mechanization and new technologies, however, never eliminated the need for longshoremen and the other maritime workers moving cargo on the waterfront. (Photograph by Richards Studio.)

Until the end of the 20th century, it was possible to drive on the Port of Tacoma Road past Eleventh Street, hang a right, and find both Johnny's Dock restaurant and Tacoma's fishing fleet and net sheds. The Port of Tacoma had established the commercial boat haven in 1953—a year before Richards took this photograph—after abandoning the idea of creating one in Old Tacoma.

Twenty years later, photographer and Croatian fisherman Ron Karabaich captured another view of the fishing fleet with salmon seiners prominent on the left. Soon both Johnny's Dock and the fleet would be gone from this site and moved to the City Waterway. Acres of containers replaced what used to be a people place.

Purex Corporation began its bleaching operations in the port-industrial area in 1950. Three months before production began, the company recruited Sunnen Crane to hoist this storage tank into its upright position on the five acres of land located near the intersection of Lincoln Avenue and Thorne Road. (Photograph by Richards Studio.)

Concrete Technology, or Concrete Engineering Company, located on Port of Tacoma Road has been manufacturing prestressed and precast concrete products since the mid-1950s. Thomas and Arthur Anderson were both president and vice president of the company and the structural engineers responsible for the long concrete construction beams that replaced those once manufactured out of wood in local lumber mills. (Photograph by Richards Studio.)

When established in 1956, Reichhold Chemicals was located on Lincoln Avenue, but within a decade, the business had moved to Taylor Way. The company manufactured chemicals needed in the expanding Pacific Northwest plywood industry. In this 1967 aerial photograph, Penn Salt is pictured in the distance. (Photograph by Richards Studio.)

Over a century before the presence of the Hibbard Stewart Company in the Port Industrial yard, the fur trade was the economic mainstay of the first Europeans. It is therefore interesting to illustrate this continuity with the modern export of hides. It is also important to note that as in the past—when Native Americans were used in the trade—non-whites, in 1970, were employed to undertake the disagreeable task of cleaning the hides. (Photograph by Richards Studio.)

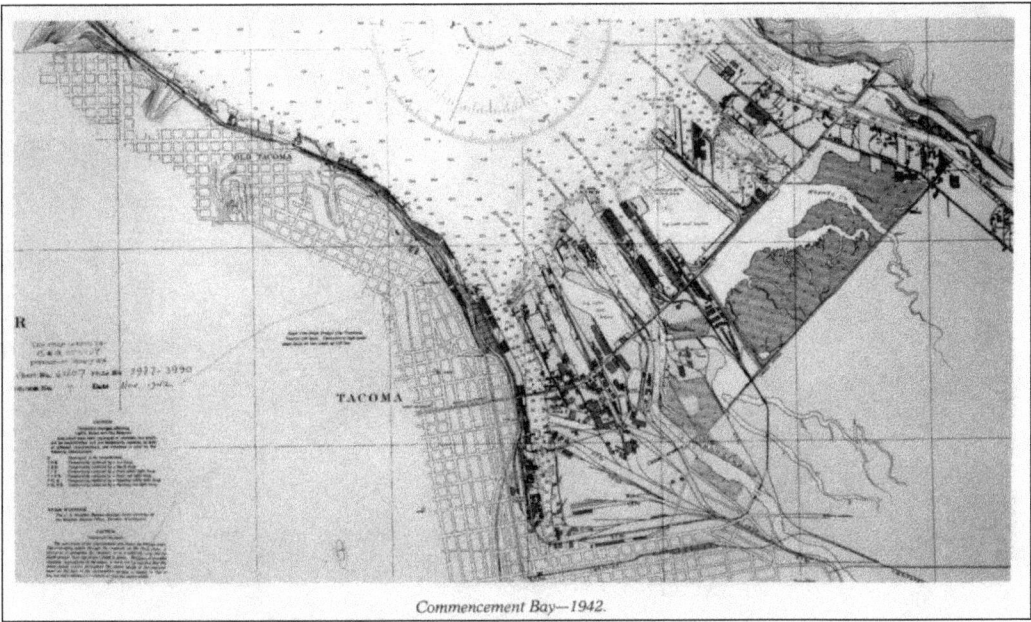

Commencement Bay—1942.

Most of the industrial and port images pictured in this chapter represent a period roughly between World War II and the 1960s. These two USGS maps drawn in 1942 and 1968 show the changes that had occurred during this time. At the outbreak of World War II, there were large parts of the original marshes that needed to be filled. In addition, not all the waterways had been dredged and log rafts were stored in the undeveloped portions. By 1968, the Blair Waterway was under construction. The Sitcum, however, was completely finished with the Keiser Aluminum dome. Most important, the marshes were now filled. As the work was underway, the Port of Tacoma commissioned aerial photographs by Richards Studio to advertise the development potential of the new land.

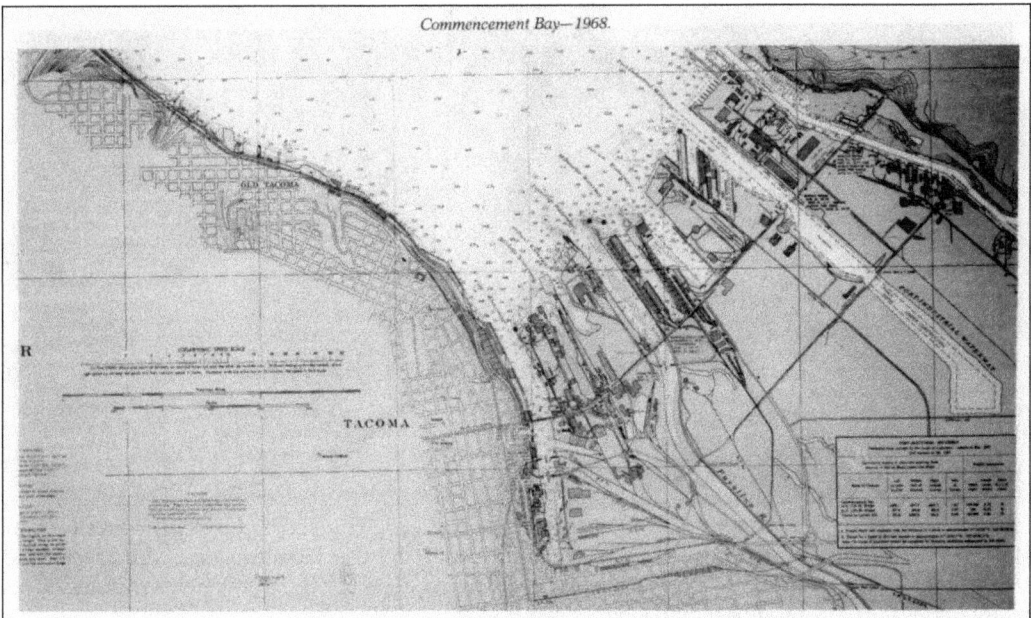

Commencement Bay—1968.

The Port of Tacoma Piers, both completed by 1923, are pictured here at a time when milled timber—piled high on Pier No. 1—dominated Tacoma's exports. Indeed, *Edmore*, the first ship to arrive at the dock in March 1921, came to load 25 carloads of timber. In 1923, Warren G. Harding was the first U.S. president to visit the facility just before his voyage to Alaska.

Fort Lewis soldiers leave Pier No. 2 in January 1940 and are transported to California for war games. The South American freighter *Coya* and (ironically) the Japanese *Koei Maru* were tied to Pier No. 1. The unfilled marshes are seen in the distance while the port's new grain elevators near completion. (Photograph by Richards Studio.)

A decade separated these two Richards aerials of the future Blair Waterway. In 1953, World War II baby flattops line the north shore of what was then the Wapato Waterway, but dredging had begun to extend it eastward. In the process, the name was changed in 1954 to honor port commissioner A. E. Blair. Within four months of this photograph, the Blair Bridge, under construction here, was completed.

By 1963, the flattops were gone and the Blair Waterway had been dredged to Lincoln Avenue. The changed port-industrial infrastructure was also beginning to reflect modern modes of transportation. Soon the Tacoma Department of Utilities' Beltline rail system would be installed to simplify what had been a classic hodgepodge of independent carriers. Roads were expanded and improved to accommodate trucks and cars.

As noted earlier, the Port of Tacoma began to aggressively promote the city's industrial potential through a series of aerial photographs taken in the early 1960s, a time when the dredging and filling of the Sitcum, Blair, and Hylebos Waterways were still underway. In 1962, for example, the intersection of Lincoln and Taylor Avenues was the focus of one view. (Lincoln runs northeast in the center of the above photograph.) Educators Manufacturing Company was the industry seen on the lower left while development awaited the eastern side of the street. Besides aerials showing available industrial space, the Port of Tacoma wanted to also show potential clients that "modern" piers were close by. In 1963, one aerial showed the Blair Waterway and emphasized the good roads and rail lines connecting industry to the port. (Photograph by Richards Studio.)

In commissioning the aerials, port authorities also wanted to show change and growth. In the above 1966 photograph by Richards, dredging of the Blair Waterway was still underway but not completed, judging from the ditch that outlined the full extent of the finished product. Eventually the undredged land would fill the marshes. Below, dredging for the Hylebos and Blair Waterways, along with the Sitcum and its Keizer Aluminum dome, were now done. The farmlands of the Puyallup Valley, the town of Fife, and Mount Rainier form a backdrop to this port-industrial masterpiece. In the distance, where the shining new concrete of I-5 comes into view, there are signs of more change to come.

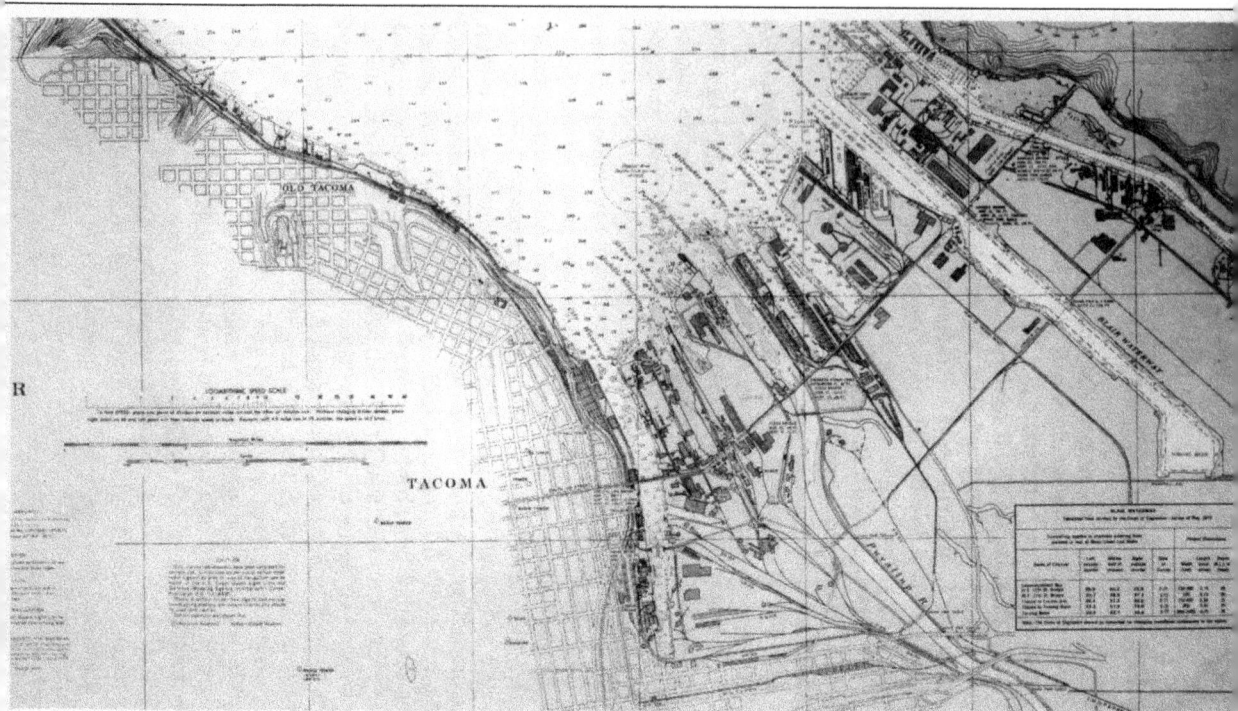

Commencement Bay—1974.

By 1974, when the USGS published this map, Tacoma's Puyallup River delta had grown from an ecology of marshes, comparable to that seen today on the Nisqually, to an intricate port complex of waterways extending into the original mudflats. The dredging provided the fill needed to create acres of land for new industry. This year was a symbolic end to the first phase of port history. The Puyallup Tribe of Indians had by this time begun to document the injustices cast upon them by early developers and were ultimately to receive compensation for the past ills of history. Port officials were also faced again with the need for change, given their role in an international trade centered on the transport of containers on freighters whose size was far larger than those of the past. So after 1974, once again, the Port of Tacoma began to redesign itself into something new and different.

Six

THE TWO POINTS

Commencement Bay was, and is, known for its deep water. The bay was not without its hazards, however. Tides running through the Narrows proved challenging to shippers navigating around Point Defiance. Even more dangerous was Browns Point, the sandy beach where George Vancouver had his spring-day salmon lunch. No one knows for sure how the point got its name; Wilkes called it Point Harris. By the time Oscar Brown, pictured in this 1939 photograph, came to tend the lighthouse in 1903, its name was a settled matter. Oscar always claimed that it was "named for an old settler" and not for him. The first lighthouse tended by Oscar Brown was a primitive wood structure that the Coast Guard replaced with this art deco one in 1934. Oscar spent 36 years tending the light. After he retired in 1939, the Coast Guard converted it to an automated system. (Photograph by Richards Studio.)

When American settlement began around Commencement Bay, Browns Point was a part of both King County and the Puyallup Indian Reservation. By 1901, however, the jurisdictional boundary had changed, and the reservation had been divided into single allotments, with Jerry Meeker (his father was named Sky-uch) the primary benefactor in the Browns Point area. By 1907, Meeker and his Tacoma business partners, had platted Hyada Park to attract those wanting to permanently settle on the north side of the bay. By the end of World War I in 1918, there were enough children for a school. A year later, the Browns Point Improvement Club formed to raise money for a piano for the school. By 1915, the community had its own volunteer fire department and proceeded to show off its new equipment for Marvin Boland and a *Tacoma News Tribune* reporter. Lighthouse keeper Oscar Brown was chief of the volunteers.

Mavis Stears, in her history of Browns and Dash Points, notes that the two communities operated the Crestview Observation Post pictured above during World War II. Volunteers watched for enemy planes from this site located on the highest area above these two points. The observation post was dedicated, turned over to the army in October 1942, and joined similar stations in Point Defiance Park. These photographs by Richards were taken as a part of the ceremonies held in the Browns Point Community Hall. Below Leona Burton (left) and Mrs. S. E. Peterson posed for the benefit of photographers.

George Vancouver's salmon lunch began his brief introduction to Browns Point so it seems only appropriate to end with the fish. Ever since 1946, when the Improvement Club needed funds for a clubhouse, the community has held a summer salmon fest. The man in the middle of this 1960 Richards view might be Edwin Swanson, chef in charge of the bake.

Food was also what visitors would encounter coming up Marine View Drive from Tacoma. In 1925, Bill Keyes opened the Cliff House Tavern on the hillside overlooking Commencement Bay. Buz Erhart later owned the tavern. Following a fire in 1958, Houston O. Smith remodeled the business into a restaurant that has survived to this day. (Photograph by Richards Studio.)

102

There were parts of Ruston Way near Point Defiance where development came slowly. Richards took the above view near the North Stevens Street end on December 28, 1936, to show the route used after 10-year-old Charles Mattson was kidnapped the night before. Police theorized that the unknown gunman carried the boy from the Mattson home, across Waterview Street and the railroad tracks to a waiting car on Ruston Way. Howard Holman owned the Bayshore Boat Lockers and adjacent house (below)—located near the Mattson site—before J. R. Wigen commissioned this 1963 photograph by Richards. The Lobster Shop now occupies the space.

The south shore of Commencement Bay from Old Tacoma to the ASARCO smelter was dominated by the sights, sounds, and smells of lumber mills and much of the industry's history was told in a separate volume on the history of Old Tacoma. Over time, there were some 25 mills operating along an expanse of two miles, beginning in 1869 with the Hanson, Ackerson Mill and ending in 1977 with the closure of Dickman Lumber Company. Economic conditions, federal regulations, and fires brought an end to the mills, including the Pacific Mill pictured in this undated Davidson photograph. This mill, along with the Tacoma Smelter that replaced it on the site, was located on the shoreline south of Point Defiance. Operators fed the mill by logging the hills surrounding it, just like all the other early Puget Sound mill owners. The activity deprived the federal government of significant revenue, but it also cleared the land for settlement or industry, in this case the construction of Dennis Ryan's smelter.

Charles Wilkes named Point Defiance in 1841 when he began his explorations on Commencement Bay. Early military planners saw its potential as a fortress, and with the support of Pres. Andrew Johnson in 1866, a military reservation was authorized by Congress, and it joined reservations at the southern tip of Vashon Island and the north shore of Gig Harbor. Collectively they were to form a triangular defensive system in the lower Sound. The plan was never implemented, and by the 1880s, Tacomans had discovered that illegal logging was taking place within the reservation. In addition, those who could manage the trip were finding their way to Point Defiance for a little bit of recreation. Soon the idea of transferring ownership of the land to the City of Tacoma for park purposes was on everyone's mind. While taken long after this time, this undated photograph shows the delight of Tacomans on a daytime visit to the park.

In 1888, with the help of Rep. Francis W. Cushman, Congress decided to let Tacoma use Point Defiance for park purposes, but years were to pass before the federal government completely relinquished its military rights to the property. That, however, did not stop Tacomans from treating the land as its own and developing what later park historians would call a pleasure ground, or a place for quiet reflection not for active playground recreation. These two undated photographs of the Point Defiance pavilion and boat landing illustrate what the concept meant for early Tacomans. Above, the results of prior logging appear behind the pavilion. Below, pleasure seekers embark from an unnamed steamer.

Automobiles, motorboats, and airplanes were to change the Commencement Bay shoreline near the point, as a new boathouse replaced the pavilion. The facility, pictured above, was designed for boat storage, although not all boats seen in this aerial view would have fit into the small stalls. The northern end of Pearl Street had become a ferry slip for automobiles and pedestrians venturing to Vashon Island. Below, in 1940, the distant land had already been prepared for moorage and a home for the Tacoma Yacht Club. The vintage seaplane would have been a rare occurrence at this time and might be the reason why an unidentified photographer captured the view.

#10 - POINT DEFIANCE PARK [ILLEGIBLE] SMOKE STACK

The history of park planning in Tacoma goes back to 1883 when Clinton Ferry donated land for a neighborhood playground. In 1907, after state legislative authorization, voters agreed to create the Metropolitan Park District of Tacoma. Point Defiance Park became the gemstone of a system that covered the city with parks and playgrounds. In 1911, the board hired the Kansas City architectural firm of Hare and Hare to create a plan that would combine places for both passive reflection and active recreation. In the process, as this undated postcard view shows, a large, grassy, gathering place and pond were placed near the park entrance. What park planners could not avoid throughout this endeavor, however, was the proximity of a smelter near the southern border of Point Defiance. Even though the smelter stack was always a reminder of industry nearby, park visitors did not at first openly object to the relationship.

The new smelter industry began innocently enough. In 1888, while Tacomans were celebrating their acquisition of Point Defiance Park, Dennis Ryan was organizing the Tacoma Milling and Smelting Company and locating his new industry just south of the future pleasure ground. As with other places around the bay, the land Ryan chose included clam beds harvested by the Puyallup Indians. Early Tacoma historian Herbert Hunt reported that a native burial site was also a part of what became the smelter landscape. Even so, Ryan began clearing the land and constructing the plant seen here. Trestled docks lead to the facility, and workers settled into housing constructed between the smelter and the park. For the next two years, Ryan produced "more smoke than profit," according to historian Murray Morgan and was therefore quite willing to sell his operations to William R. Rust's Tacoma Smelting and Refining Company.

William Rust rebuilt the smelter and fired up the furnaces in September 1890. By the end of the month, the *Queen of the Pacific* was sailing to San Francisco with 23 tons of processed bullion worth some $10,000. Even though taken in 1900, the smelter looked much like this when Rust proved it a success a decade before.

The unidentified group of men posed here were the Tacoma Smelter workers in 1900. Like many others linked to the mining industry, there were no unions and would not be any for years to come. Most of the men lived in Ruston, a town adjacent to the mill and built on land owned by Tacoma Smelter investors. Many workers were Croatian immigrants.

The Tacoma Smelter was one of the few Tacoma industries that survived the 1893 depression, and in the process, William Rust opened a pathway towards ultimate outside ownership and control. "With the return of prosperity in the late nineties," explained Murray Morgan, "he enlisted the support of . . . Darius Odgen Mills, a power in mining financing." Through the influence of Mills, more mine owners knocked on Rust's door so that by 1905, five years after the above photograph was taken, the Tacoma Smelter had been expanded to include the first Pacific Coast electrolytic copper refinery. Below, workers posed in front of the newly modernized complex.

With a modern plant growing out of the old, and East Coast investors having their collective foot in the door, Rust and the Tacoma Smelter became part of a high stakes Wall Street game involving the Guggenheim brothers, who had just acquired effective control of the American Smelting and Refining Company (ASARCO). Negotiations began to convince Rust to sell to the brothers, something he was willing to do if the price was right. Wall Street wizard Bernard Baruch, along with Rust and other members of the Guggenheim team, agreed upon a $5.5 million price with Rust remaining general manager. The timing was perfect for the brothers. World War I was on the not-too-distant horizon, and America's entry into the hostilities corresponded to another smelter—now ASARCO—round of modernization. As for William Rust, he received a bonus from Bernard Baruch for his cooperation and used it to build his mansion on North I Street.

One symbol of the new ASARCO was the 571-foot chimney pictured here in a 1917 photograph by Richards. For workers, it soon became a symbol of corporate power waging war against them, especially the unskilled that wanted to organize. Labor strikes had been underway since 1912. When granted wage increases were cut in 1914—smelter improvements were underway by this time—workers struck again on January 1, this time with the support of the longshoremen. The hill behind the smelter stack, seen in the background of this view, became a battleground as workers fired into the yard from a house. When Pierce County sheriff Jamieson threatened to "turn all rifles on that house" and turn it into a "pepper box," workers used a large slingshot to toss rocks into the smelter yard. One young worker was killed, and the issues of union recognition and wages were not resolved at this time.

In 1935, the *Tacoma Times* commissioned Richards to photograph smelter operations for a January issue of the newspaper. By this time, the smaller smelter stack seen in the 1917 photograph was gone, and a trestled conveyor led to the remaining one. The Northern Pacific tunneled underneath the stack when rerouting its line through Point Defiance. Streets were now graded. One paralleled the railroad and led to Ruston Way and the shoreline. The other took workers to Ruston and Tacoma neighborhoods. The ASARCO stack had become a multifaceted symbol by this time. For King County residents, the structure was a curse as the south winds blew the refining residues—especially arsenic—northward. For ship operators, the height of the stack made it a perfect navigation beacon. Tacomans, conveniently forgetting that the industry was located outside its urban boundaries, lauded the company's economic contribution to the city.

The Town of Ruston, including the smelter, incorporated in 1906, a year after William Rust sold the refinery to ASARCO, and he had platted smelter-owned land into lots sold or rented to workers. From the very beginning, Rust was adamant about not having his development a part of the city of Tacoma. A few houses are seen in the foreground of this undated aerial photograph. In 1914, striking workers fired from the hill to the right.

Looking southward around 1961, Richards was able to capture much of the south shore of Commencement Bay from the smelter to Old Tacoma. The ever-present refinery pollution constantly plagued ASARCO officials until the decision was made in 1984 to cease operations. On a cold winter day in 1993, thousands of cameras aimed toward the point to capture the implosion of the stack and its collapse to the ground.

Because of the need to protect industrial secrets, ASARCO officials allowed few interior or exterior photographs showing what went on at Ruston. Besides the stack, shipping wharves, and slag piles, there were, for example, a metallic arsenic area, arsenic kitchens, and arsenic roasters, along with an acid plant building and a sodium dioxide plant. Close to Point Defiance Park, there were reverberatory furnaces, oil tanks, refineries, and settling/evaporation basins. Anode furnaces and a nickel plant shared the shoreline with the shipping wharf. The waste-heat boilers was one interior view that Richards was permitted to photograph in 1939. A group of workers are dwarfed by what appears as a work of modern industrial art encompassing metal framework, tanks, and curved pipes working their way into the floor.

Tacoma Times reporter J. Guis was able to use these two interior photographs taken by Richards in his January 19, 1935, article. Above, 2,700-degree molten liquid ore is flowing from the smelter reverbatory furnace. Below, an unidentified worker is manipulating the operations of an unknown process. In 1933, under the encouragement of the International Union of Mine, Mill, and Smelter Workers, the men organized Smeltermen's Local 25. Unlike the maritime and lumber unions, whose strikes had paralyzed the port, the smeltermen were able, in September 1933, to negotiate a 25¢ wage increase. Serious strike activity did not occur until 1946, when men nationwide walked out of ASARCO plants.

Smelting was a process involving the import of raw materials and the export of the refined product within the context of an international economy. While the sources for ore varied with time, Rust first obtained them from the Treadwell Mine in Juneau, Alaska, as well as additional mines in the Coeur d'Alenes of Idaho. He also owned the Pierce County town of Fairfax where the workers mined coal to fuel the smelter operations, at least until replaced with newer power sources. By 1935, imported ore was mechanically hoisted from ship to hopper using what were then state-of-the-art cranes, with each one able to lift five tons of ore from the hold during a haul. At left, a crane operator demonstrated one part of its operation. Below, the crane is dumping ore into a hopper. (Photograph by Richards Studio.)

In 1933, smelting in Tacoma received a boost when the United States diplomatically recognized the Soviet Union. At this time, Russia mined 15.6 percent of the world's gold ore but lacked the technology and infrastructure to refine it. In this 1935 Richards view, Russian ore in an unidentified European ship is being unloaded at the Tacoma ASARCO dock.

Tragedy met the smelter in 1938 when Fred Birkby was killed while riding a train that was dumping slag into Commencement Bay. According to the *Tacoma Times*, a locomotive and six cars carrying the molten material—along with Birkby—were thrown into the water when the loose slag pile underneath the tracks collapsed.

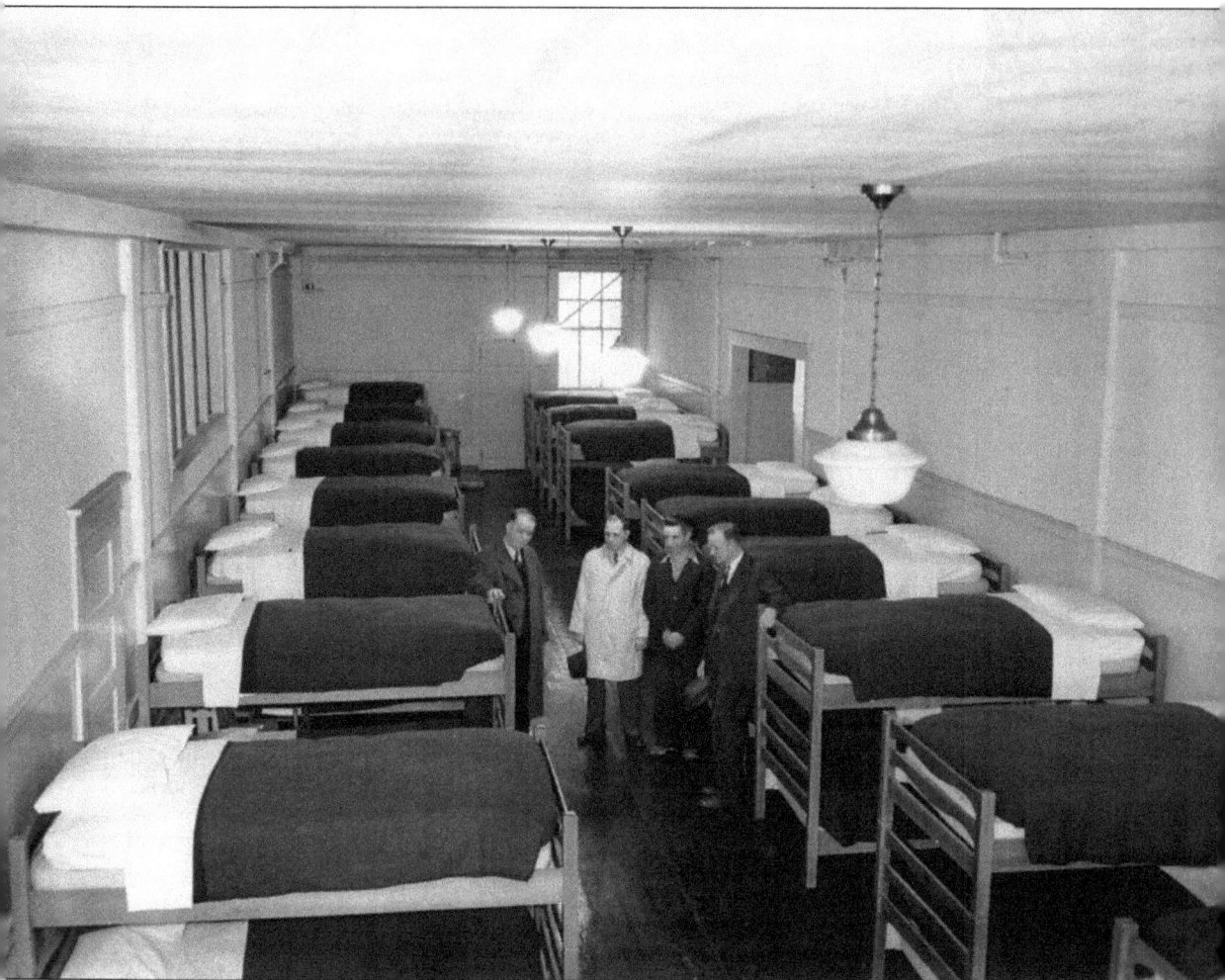

Both world wars brought an influx of single men and families to Tacoma to work. During World War I, for example, the city experienced the arrival of African Americans who migrated north to take advantage of employment opportunities unavailable in the southern states. Housing then, as during World War II, was a constant problem, especially for single men. ASARCO was able to solve the dilemma during the latter war with the help of the Tacoma Housing Authority. This Depression-era agency constructed a 60-bed facility called the Ruston Terrace Dormitory at North Fifty-first and Winifred. Officials of the Tacoma Housing Authority inspect the complete facility in 1943. Pictured here by the bunks, from left to right, are chairman of the authority Fred Shoemaker, Harold Bergerson, manager of the dormitory Leo Wingard, and W. C. Taplin. (Photograph by Richards Studio.)

Ruston, like Old Tacoma, its sister neighborhood to the south, had its fair share of characters. Ole "Chicken" Olson was one whose story made it into the pages of the *Tacoma Times* in July 1944. Ole was 73 years old and lived in this house and "farm" at 5007 North Highland Avenue. His home, according to complaining neighbors, included a menagerie of pigeons, rabbits, chickens, pigs, maybe a goat, and cats, including the one that joined him in the portrait pictured below. According to the story, the sheriff, with the support of the neighborhood, placed Ole under a guardianship, and he was given a year to clean up the place.

As home for most of the ASARCO workers, Ruston deserves a history of its own. This Richards view (and the one pictured at the bottom of the page) serves as a reminder that the town was a neighborhood of families. In 1928, Ruston principal and coach Mrs. Lou Miller (left) and Gertrude Tenzler posed with the school's track team. Richard Anderson (first row, far right) and John Slavich (back row, third from right) are the only identified boys.

Bowling was a sport for Ruston women, and community lanes were provided for the recreation. These wives or daughters of ASARCO workers were champions of the Ruston Bowling League in 1943. From left to right, the winners were Grace Murphy, Lena Larsen, Lois Oberg, and Margaret Velacich.

Seven

AFTERWORD

As originally conceived, this history was to include a single chapter on the men and women who worked the waterfront. The expanse of the story was so complex, however, that the authors concluded that the history of shoreline labor deserves separate attention. Even so, workers made Tacoma's ever-changing port, and this afterword is to provide a hint of their story. Part of it is political, as in 1936, when both lumber workers and longshoremen demonstrated their support for the reelection of Pres. Franklin D. Roosevelt. The rally began at Union Station at Nineteenth Street and Pacific Avenue and wound its way to the Greenwich Coliseum on Thirteenth Street and Fawcett Avenue. Workers knew the building well, for besides political rallies, it was also a popular dance hall and sports arena. On this night in October, however, the workers listened to the likes of Sen. Lewis B. Schwellenbach along with an assorted collection of local Democrat politicos. (Photograph by Richards Studio.)

The *Tacoma News Tribune* referred to these 1947 protestors as members of the Smelter Workers Union, and teenage Communist sympathizers gathered to protest the Temple Theater appearance of Republican senator and presidential hopeful Robert A. Taft. Two years before Richards photographed the gathering, the Soviet Union was America's ally. Now protestors were expressing their opposition to Taft's charge that Pres. Harry Truman was soft on Communism.

Also in 1947, the United Steel Workers of America commissioned a series of photographs showing employees at Permanente Metals, including these two unidentified men. (The company was located at 3400 Taylor Way.) The union had been formed in 1936, when Phillip Murray, then vice president of the United Mine Workers, became chairman of the organizing committee.

124

Roosevelt supported nationwide union organization, and before his campaign visit, the 1930s witnessed two major strikes that rattled the waterfront. The combined longshore and lumber handlers unions walked off the docks in May 1934 over issues of recognition, hiring practices, wages, and working conditions. Unlike a lumber workers strike called a year later, pictured here in a Chapin Bowen photograph, Gov. Clarence Martin did not call out the National Guard against the maritime workers when strikers threatened a general strike, because the guards own "Flying Squad" kept scabs at bay. The maritime strike, one that covered the entire Pacific Coast, was eventually settled by arbitration in July 1934. On May 6, 1935, lumber workers walked out of the forests and mills for reasons comparable to the longshoremen, and in opposition to the company-run Loyal Legion of Loggers and Lumbermen. Unlike the longshoremen, however, lumber workers could not prevent the hiring of scabs or the arrival of the National Guard, pictured here boarding trucks on the port side of the Eleventh Street Bridge.

The mill owners, not local authorities, requested the presence of the National Guard. Indeed, Pierce County sheriff Jack Bjorklund, a former longshore union official, refused to "prostitute his principles" by supporting such an action. However, the guard's presence did not break the strike since local longshoremen refused to handle scab lumber. The best the military could do was to try to keep the striking lumbermen out of the port-industrial area by establishing an Eleventh Street Bridge blockade in downtown Tacoma. On July 12, matters turned ugly as demonstrating strikers and the National Guard met head-on. Photographer Chapin Bowen captured the event as strikers tossed back the tear gas canisters thrown at them, and the guard destroyed one of their trucks by trying to shoot the gas through its exhaust system. Tacomans became outraged as the guard bloodied heads, beat picketers, and stationed men with fixed bayonets on every downtown street corner.

As with the maritime unions, federal mediators were used to end the lumber workers' strike, and by August 1935, men, such as these returning to the St. Paul and Tacoma Lumber Company, went back to work. In concluding his history of the maritime strike, historian Ron Magden noted that the endeavor allowed the men to gain "a sense of power and solidarity . . . that carried their unions to further victories in future negotiations." The same can be said for the lumber workers. In both instances, mediation and compromise ended the labor actions. The willingness of both sides to yield is a crucial point to make as this history ends. The expansion of Tacoma's shoreline from the Northern Pacific's first shipping wharves in 1873 to today's port-industrial area has always been dependent upon the cooperative effort of both employer and employee. It is a relationship that continues to breathe life into Tacoma's working waterfront.

Visit us at
arcadiapublishing.com